Web Corpus Construction

Synthesis Lectures on Human Language Technologies

Editor
Graeme Hirst, *University of Toronto*

Synthesis Lectures on Human Language Technologies is edited by Graeme Hirst of the University of Toronto. The series consists of 50- to 150-page monographs on topics relating to natural language processing, computational linguistics, information retrieval, and spoken language understanding. Emphasis is on important new techniques, on new applications, and on topics that combine two or more HLT subfields.

Web Corpus Construction
Roland Schäfer and Felix Bildhauer
2013

Recognizing Textual Entailment: Models and Applications
Ido Dagan, Dan Roth, Mark Sammons, and Fabio Massimo Zanzotto
2013

Semi-Supervised Learning and Domain Adaptation in Natural Language Processing
Anders Søgaard
2013

Linguistic Fundamentals for Natural Language Processing: 100 Essentials from Morphology and Syntax
Emily M. Bender
2013

Semantic Relations Between Nominals
Vivi Nastase, Preslav Nakov, Diarmuid Ó Séaghdha, and Stan Szpakowicz
2013

Computational Modeling of Narrative
Inderjeet Mani
2012

Natural Language Processing for Historical Texts
Michael Piotrowski
2012

Introduction to Chinese Natural Language Processing
Kam-Fai Wong, Wenjie Li, Ruifeng Xu, and Zheng-sheng Zhang
2009

Introduction to Linguistic Annotation and Text Analytics
Graham Wilcock
2009

Dependency Parsing
Sandra Kübler, Ryan McDonald, and Joakim Nivre
2009

Statistical Language Models for Information Retrieval
ChengXiang Zhai
2008

Web Corpus Construction
Roland Schäfer and Felix Bildhauer

ISBN: 978-3-031-01024-8   paperback
ISBN: 978-3-031-02152-7   ebook

DOI 10.1007/978-3-031-02152-7

A Publication in the Springer series
SYNTHESIS LECTURES ON HUMAN LANGUAGE TECHNOLOGIES

Lecture #22
Series Editor: Graeme Hirst, *University of Toronto*
Series ISSN
Synthesis Lectures on Human Language Technologies
Print 1947-4040   Electronic 1947-4059

Web Corpus Construction

Roland Schäfer and Felix Bildhauer
Freie Universität Berlin

SYNTHESIS LECTURES ON HUMAN LANGUAGE TECHNOLOGIES #22

ABSTRACT

The World Wide Web constitutes the largest existing source of texts written in a great variety of languages. A feasible and sound way of exploiting this data for linguistic research is to compile a static corpus for a given language. There are several advantages of this approach: (i) Working with such corpora obviates the problems encountered when using Internet search engines in quantitative linguistic research (such as non-transparent ranking algorithms). (ii) Creating a corpus from web data is virtually free. (iii) The size of corpora compiled from the WWW may exceed by several orders of magnitudes the size of language resources offered elsewhere. (iv) The data is locally available to the user, and it can be linguistically post-processed and queried with the tools preferred by her/him.

This book addresses the main practical tasks in the creation of web corpora up to giga-token size. Among these tasks are the sampling process (i. e., web crawling) and the usual cleanups including boilerplate removal and removal of duplicated content. Linguistic processing and problems with linguistic processing coming from the different kinds of noise in web corpora are also covered. Finally, the authors show how web corpora can be evaluated and compared to other corpora (such as traditionally compiled corpora).

For additional material please visit the companion website

http://sites.morganclaypool.com/wcc

KEYWORDS

corpus creation, web corpora, web crawling, web characterization, boilerplate removal, language identification, duplicate detection, near-duplicate detection, tokenization, POS tagging, noisy data, corpus evaluation, corpus comparison, keyword extraction

Contents

Preface

Our approach to the subject of web corpus construction is guided by our own practical experience in the area. Coming from an empirically oriented linguistics background, we required large amounts of data for empirical research in various languages, including more or less non-standard language. However, we noticed that, depending on the research question and the language of interest, appropriate text resources are not always available and/or freely accessible and in the appropriate form (cf. Section 1 for examples). Therefore, we took the work by the WaCky initiative [Baroni et al., 2009] and the Leipzig Corpora Collection (LCC, Biemann et al., 2007; Goldhahn et al., 2012) as a starting point to build our own large corpora from web data, leading to the development of the `texrex` software suite and the COW ("COrpora from the web") corpora.[1,2]

We dealt with the usual technical problems in web corpus construction, like boilerplate removal and deduplication, noticing that there was no concise and reasonably complete introductory textbook on these technicalities available, although there are overview articles like Fletcher [2011]; Kilgarriff and Grefenstette [2003]; Lüdeling et al. [2007]. Additionally, it became clear to us that even the mere use of web corpora for linguistic research requires extra precautions and more in-depth knowledge about the corpus construction process compared to the use of established and "clean" corpus resources. This knowledge—mostly specific to web corpora—includes important matters like:

- How was the corpus material sampled, which in this case means "crawled"?
- Which parts of the documents are removed in the usual "cleaning" steps, and with which accuracy?
- Which documents are removed completely by which criteria, for example, near-duplicate documents?
- What kinds of noise are present in the data itself (e. g., misspellings), and what was normalized, removed, etc., by the corpus designers?
- Which kinds of noise might be introduced by the post-processing, such as tokenization errors, inaccurate POS tagging, etc.?

The literature on these subjects comes to some extent (or rather to a large extent) from the search engine and data mining sphere, as well as from Computational Linguistics. It is also quite diverse, and no canonical set of papers has been established yet, making it difficult to get a complete picture in a short time. We hope to have compiled an overview of the papers which can be considered recommended readings for anyone who wishes to compile a web corpus using their

---

[1]http://sourceforge.net/projects/texrex/
[2]http://www.corporafromtheweb.org/

own tools (own crawlers, boilerplate detectors, deduplication software, etc.) or using available tools.[3] Equally important is our second goal, namely that this tutorial puts any web corpus user in a position to make educated use of the available resources.

Although the book is primarily intended as a tutorial, this double goal and the extremely diverse background which might be required leads to a mix of more practical and more theoretical sections. Especially, Chapter 2 on data collection contains the least amount of practical recommendation, mainly because data collection (primarily: web crawling) has—in our perception— received the least attention (in terms of fundamental research) within the web corpus construction community. Chapters 3 on non-linguistic post-processing and 4 on linguistic post-processing are probably the most practical chapters. Chapter 5 briefly touches upon the question of how we can assess the quality of a web corpus (mainly by comparing it to other corpora). Thus, it is of high theoretical relevance while containing concrete recommendations regarding some methods which can be used.

Roland Schäfer and Felix Bildhauer
July 2013

---

[3]We make some software recommendations, but strictly from the open source world. We do this not so much out of dogmatism, but rather because there are open source variants of all important tools and libraries available, and nobody has to pay for the relevant software.

Acknowledgments

Much of the material in this book was presented as a foundational course at the European Summer School in Logic, Language and Information (ESSLLI) 2012 in Opole, Poland, by the authors. We would like to thank the ESSLLI organizers for giving us the chance to teach the course. We also thank the participants of the ESSLLI course for their valuable feedback and discussion, especially Ekaterina Chernyak (NRU-HSE, Moscow, Russia). Also, we are grateful for many comments by participants of diverse talks, presentations, and workshops held between 2011 and 2013. Furthermore, we would like to thank Adam Kilgarriff and two anonymous reviewers for detailed and helpful comments on a draft version of this book. Any errors, omissions, and inadequacies which remain are probably due to us not listening to all these people.

We could not have written this tutorial without our prior work on our own corpora and tools. Therefore, we thank Stefan Müller (Freie Universität Berlin) for allowing us to stress the computing infrastructure of the German Grammar work group to its limits. We also thank the GNU/Linux support team at the *Zedat* data centre of Freie Universität Berlin for their technical support (Robert Schüttler, Holger Weiß, and many others). Finally, we thank our student research assistant, Sarah Dietzfelbinger, for doing much of the dirty work (like generating training data for classifiers).

The second author's work on this book was funded by the *Deutsche Forschungsgemeinschaft*, SFB 632 "Information Structure," Project A6.

Roland Schäfer would like to thank his parents for substantial support in a critical phase of the writing of this book.

Felix Bildhauer is very much indebted to Chiaoi and Oskar for their patience and support while he was working on this book.

Roland Schäfer and Felix Bildhauer
July 2013

CHAPTER 1

Web Corpora

Although corpus-based Linguistics has seen a rise in popularity over the past few decades, for many research questions the available resources are sometimes too small, sometimes too unbalanced, or they are balanced according to inappropriate criteria for the task, sometimes too close to the respective standard language (again, for certain types of research questions), and sometimes they are simply too expensive. Sometimes, it is also the case that the interfaces provided to access available corpora are too restricted in search or export options to do serious quantitative research or use the corpus for Computational Linguistics tasks. In addition, many freely available corpora cannot be downloaded as a whole, which is required for many applications in Computational Linguistics. Examples of the above include:

- The German *Deutsches Referenzkorpus* (DeReKo; Kupietz et al., 2010) by the *Institut für Deutsche Sprache* (IDS) is large (currently over 5 billion words), but it contains predominantly newspaper text and is therefore unsuitable for research which requires a corpus containing a variety of registers, genres, etc.
- The corpus by the *Digitales Wörterbuch der Deutschen Sprache* (DWDS; Geyken, 2006) is a carefully balanced corpus of the German language of the 20th century, optimized for lexicographic research. However, it contains only 123 million tokens. On top of the small size, export options are highly limited, and many texts in the corpus are not licensed for export by non-project members.[1]
- Most of this is true for the British National Corpus (BNC; Leech, 1993).
- The corpora distributed by the Linguistic Data Consortium are small and expensive. They often add huge value through rich annotation, but while this is extremely useful for some types of research, in some areas researchers need corpora several orders of magnitude larger. E. g., the Penn Treebank [Marcus et al., 1993, 1999] contains roughly 4.5 million words and costs $3,150 at the time of this writing according to the web page.[2]
- The French Frantext corpus, provided by *Analyse et Traitement Informatique de la Langue Française* (ATILF), is a collection consisting predominantly of fictional texts and philosophical literature.[3,4] As of early 2013, it comprises slightly over four thousand documents

---

[1]Since any criticism regarding the specific composition of balanced corpora is guided by individual scientific needs and therefore futile, we will not engage in it.

[2]http://ldc.upenn.edu/

[3]http://www.frantext.fr/

[4]http://www.atilf.fr/

(the providers do not publish any token counts on the website), ranging from the 12th to 21st century (and including 850 texts from 1950 or later).

- The Spanish *Corpus de Referencia del Español Actual* (CREA) by *Academia Real Española* contains 155 million tokens and is a balanced corpus of predominantly written language from many different Spanish-speaking countries. Access through a WWW interface is free, but the query language is rather limited, there are bugs in the query engine, the display options are limited, and query results cannot be exported.

- The Spanish *Corpus del Español* [Davies, 2002] is offered with an advanced query interface and contains texts from the 13th to the 20th centuries which sum up to 100 million word tokens. However, contemporary Spanish (20th century) is represented by a mere 20 million tokens.

- The Swedish *Språkbanken* project at *Göteborgs Universitet* offers free access to roughly 1 billion tokens through a web interface.[5] It is thus quite large. However, it cannot be downloaded as a whole.

In Theoretical Linguistics, researchers sometimes try to obviate limitations of available resources through Googleology. Especially when data on low-frequency or non-standard phenomena is needed, search engine queries (mostly using Google's service) are used to look for single occurrences of some grammatical construction, or—even worse—result counts returned for such queries are used for more or less formal statistical inference. This must be considered bad science by any account. Everything that needs to be said about Googleology was already said in Kilgarriff [2006]. Problems with Googleology include, but are not restricted to:

1. Search engines are designed to favor precision over recall [Manning et al., 2009, 432] according to non-linguistic relevance criteria. This means that we can never be sure that we have found all or even some of the linguistically relevant results.

2. The ranking criteria are not known exactly, although usually variants of PageRank-like measures [Brin and Page, 1998] are used (cf. Section 2.4.2). Ranking can even be influenced by economical factors (sponsored ranking). For good research practice, some form or random sampling from the corpus would be required.

3. Search engines adapt the ranking of the results according to information like the language of the browser or the headers sent by the client which inform the server about the user's preferred language, geo-location of the client's IP address, etc. In practice, this means that two identical queries almost never result in the same results being displayed, which makes any claim based on these results non-reproducible—a clear indication of bad science.

4. Search engines expand and reduce search terms without providing feedback about the exact nature of the expansions and reductions. This includes methods like spelling correction and morphological analysis [Cucerzan and Brill, 2004]. Queries are also optimized, e. g., by bracketing sub-expressions of the original query in order to improve the overall precision.

[5]http://spraakbanken.gu.se/

Such methods are often based on analyses of query logs [Guo et al., 2008; Hagen et al., 2011; Risvik et al., 2003]. Especially if we take query result counts to make quantitative statements, we do not know even remotely what kind of (expanded or reduced) queries they actually represent.

5. Despite performing a lot of such covert linguistic processing, search engines offer no linguistic annotation. Controlled wildcarding (including wildcarding over parts-of-speech or lemmata) is not available. This means that we cannot apply the usual search heuristics required to find all relevant examples in a corpus.

6. Search engines return estimated total counts, which fluctuate on a daily basis. A few papers, such as Eu [2008] and recently Rayson et al. [2012] discuss this fluctuation and its impact on linguistic research. In Rayson et al. [2012], a method is suggested to derive stable frequencies from fluctuating search engine counts through long-term observation. It is stated that more advanced time series statistics could provide even better results. The counts would still depend on which documents the search engine considers worth indexing, and the practical feasibility compared to the use of a static web corpus needs to be proven.

7. In any case, counts returned by search engines are usually page counts, not token counts. Whether the number of web pages on which a term or expression occurs is relevant at all is a very open question (but see Keller and Lapata, 2003, who find a high correlation between the counts returned by search engines and frequencies in traditional corpora like the BNC).

8. The "corpus" which is indexed by a search engine (some part of the indexable web deemed relevant by the search engine provider) changes frequently, including the massive creation of new pages and the removal of old ones. To deal with this, the index of a search engine is constantly updated, but different pages are re-indexed at quite different intervals. This means that pseudo-scientific results obtained from search engines cannot be reproduced by other researchers. Even if all other points of criticism put forward here were invalid, this single fact makes reporting search engine results bad science.

To avoid such problems with search engine results and to fill the gaps left by available traditionally compiled corpora, web corpora as popularized by the WaCky initiative [Baroni et al., 2009] or the Leipzig Corpora Collection (LCC, Biemann et al., 2007) are an ideal solution. If available traditional or web corpora do not suffice, then a web corpus can in principle be compiled by any researcher ad hoc and according to specific design decisions. The Leipzig Corpora are available in many languages, but for legal reasons, only sentence-wise shuffled versions are published, which makes them inappropriate for any research at the document-level. The WaCky corpora are considerably larger and contain whole documents, but they are only available for a handful of European languages. In some cases, even larger corpora than the WaCky corpora might be required.

To summarize, the main advantages of web corpora are:

1. They can be constructed at no cost beyond expenses for hard drive space, CPU power, and bandwidth.

2. They can reach almost arbitrary sizes, far in the giga-token region.

3. Entirely new registers and genres are available exclusively in web corpora (blogs, forums, etc.). Some of these genres cover texts which are much closer to spontaneous (although not necessarily spoken) language than texts contained in traditionally compiled corpora.

4. They are available locally for all kinds of processing using standard tools, database systems, etc., such that the user is not bound by the limitations of some query interface.

5. web corpus construction allows for a form of random sampling from the population of web documents (even uniform sampling, where each document has the same chance of being sampled). Furthermore, the population of web documents is very large and extremely diverse in terms of genres, styles, etc. Constructing truly random samples from such a huge and diverse population is not possible by means of traditional corpus construction. Corpora constructed in such a way could therefore be a valuable addition to available resources based on stratified sampling (i. e., balanced corpora).

The advantages have to be balanced against the disadvantages:

1. The copyright situation is unclear in some countries where there is no fair use policy (like Germany). Especially the redistribution of the corpora is problematic under such conditions.

2. Although there are advanced methods to clean web corpora, they still contain significant amounts of noisy data, such as spam web pages, redundant auto-generated content from content management systems, misspellings, etc. Compared to users of traditional corpora, users of web corpora must therefore be more aware of the steps which were taken in the construction of the corpus, such that they are aware of potential distortions of their results. As an example which will be explained in detail in Chapters 4 and 5 the word type count for web corpora is usually much too high to be plausible due to a large amount of noisy material, such that naïvely drawn statistical conclusions might be invalid.

Since web corpora can serve many different purposes, it is probably impossible to satisfy everyone with one single introductory text book. We look at the subject mainly from the point of view of empirical linguistics, which is why we kept some sections shorter than computational linguists probably would have. For example, this is certainly true for Section 2.4.3 about focused crawling (the task of mining the web for documents about certain topics, in certain languages, etc.). In making such decisions, we mainly adopted the following guideline in order to stay compatible with non-computational linguists: If there are available tools which solve a task without requiring that the user have advanced programming skills, we deal with it in detail, otherwise we discuss it briefly and include suggestions for further reading. Creating and running a focused crawler is definitely a task that requires advanced programming skills, and we therefore kept the section about it comparatively short.

Throughout the book, we will be suggesting that certain technical decisions are actually design decisions, because they influence the features of the final corpus. This is especially crucial because web corpus construction (as understood here) is a process which must usually be fully automated due to the size of the corpora. All automatic processing alters the original data, it comes with a certain error rate, and it might decrease the quality of the data instead of increasing it. This concerns the tasks of removing duplicate documents, removing design elements (menus, copyright strings, etc.) from web pages, and other cleanup and processing procedures. A good example is removal of duplication. If it is performed at the paragraph level instead of the document level, single documents will end up being incomplete in the final corpus. For some researchers, this might simply not be acceptable. Given the diverse applications of web corpora, users have to make the design decisions themselves, based on our description of how the procedures work.

We have divided the book into four main chapters. Each chapter covers a major topic in web corpus construction, and they are ordered in the usual order of practical corpus construction. Chapter 2 describes the theory and technology of data collection (crawling). Chapter 3 provides the non-linguistic cleansing which is usually applied to the collected data. Chapter 4 discusses the problems which arise in the linguistic processing (tokenizing and annotations like POS tagging) of web data. Finally, Chapter 5 introduces some methods of determining the quality of the compiled corpora.

r

CHAPTER 2

Data Collection

2.1 INTRODUCTION

In this book, we consider a web corpus to be a static collection of a number of documents downloaded from the World Wide Web (or WWW or just web). Some aspects which we discuss are only relevant if the web corpus to be constructed is intended for work in empirical Linguistics or Computational Linguistics. Clearly, data collection and post-processing for search engine applications partially require different strategies. While in search engine applications the primary goal is to find and index documents relevant to user search queries, documents in a web corpus should meet the linguistic criteria set by the corpus designers. Also, while search engines' databases are kept up to date by constantly refreshing (re-crawling) the data, a web corpus should (at least for linguistic research) not change in order to allow for reproducible corpus experiments. Since there are probably as many sets of design criteria for corpora in linguistic research as there are researchers in the field, we try to lay out the relevant knowledge and the necessary procedures such that any linguist or computational linguist is put in a position to decide upon a method of designing their corpus.

In this chapter, we discuss the acquisition of the raw data, which is the first crucial step in web corpus construction, under these premises. The properties of the final corpus is the sum of the properties of these web documents minus the documents/properties lost/changed in the post-processing steps to be outlined in later chapters. Therefore, it is crucial to give some attention to the structure of the web and the methods which we use to discover the documents (i. e., crawling). The structure of the web is briefly described in Section 2.2. Crawling is covered in greater detail in Sections 2.3.2 through 2.4. Due to the practical goals of this book, the amount of theoretical considerations is kept at a minimum. However, it cannot be avoided that this chapter is the least practical of all, mainly because data collection for web corpus construction has received the least amount of attention from the linguistic community. A more thorough but still very accessible introduction to most topics of this chapter can be found in Chapters 19–21 of Manning et al. [2009]. A more detailed introduction to crawling is Olston and Najork [2010].[1]

Having read through this chapter, readers should:

---

[1]We ignore incremental crawling (strategies of re-crawling pages at certain intervals to check whether they still exist and to refresh a search engine index) in this book, simply because it is very specific to search engine-related crawling. Since web corpora are static resources according to our definition, incremental crawling does not make sense. It is covered in Chapter 5 of Olston and Najork [2010].

1. know about the structure of the web and which web pages they can expect to find through web crawling,
2. be able to find sources from which they can obtain the URLs needed to start a crawl,
3. know how to configure available crawler software such that they download and store mostly relevant documents without putting too much strain on the servers from which they request the documents.

Secondarily, readers are made aware of the following advanced topics, which we do not cover exhaustively, though:

1. how crawling strategies affect the sample taken from the web graph,
2. where they can look for further information regarding more advanced and intelligent crawling strategies which allow predictions about the language, the contents, etc., of documents not yet downloaded.

2.2   THE STRUCTURE OF THE WEB

2.2.1   GENERAL PROPERTIES

The most remarkable feature of the web is its connectedness, the fact that it contains so-called hypertext—a concept described as early as 1989 in Berners-Lee [1989]. Essentially, this means that it contains documents, and that these documents link to each other. Each link takes the form of a Uniform Resource Locator (URL) which specifies the transfer protocol in most cases as either http:// or https://. Let $I(p)$ be the set of pages linking to p and $O(p)$ the set of pages linked to by p, then the in-degree $ID(p)$ of p is simply $|I(p)|$, the out-degree $OD(p)$ is $|O(p)|$.[2] I. e., each page has a number (possibly 0) of pages to which it links—its out-degree OD— and a number (possibly 0) of documents by which it is linked—its in-degree ID. Links cannot be followed backward, and the web graph is thus a directed cyclic graph. The in-degrees of pages are empirically distributed according to a Pareto distribution or power law with 2.1 being reported for the α parameter [Manning et al., 2009, 426]. (But see Section 2.2.3 and especially Figure 2.3 for more details on the α parameter.) For the proportion $P(i)$ of pages having in-degree i, we have:

$$P(i) = \frac{1}{i^{2.1}} = i^{-2.1} \tag{2.1}$$

In terms of network theory, this distribution of links makes the World Wide Web a scale-free network, as opposed to a random network.[3] So, there is a relatively small number of pages with a very high in-degree and a large number of pages with a low in-degree. Pages with a high in-degree are comparatively easy to find by following links from other pages. However, they are not necessarily the best pages to download for web corpus construction. Part of Section 2.4 is

---

[2]The terms *(web) page* and *(web) document* are used interchangeably here.
[3]An accessible introduction to scale-free networks is Barabási and Bonabeau [2003].

devoted to the task of optimizing the document discovery process toward exploring pages with low in-degrees.

In an early paper, Broder et al. [2000] divided the web into various components, based on how they are connected. Broder et al. introduced what is called the bowtie structure of the web (Fig. 2.1).

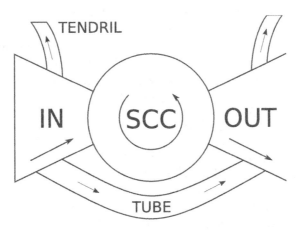

Figure 2.1: Simplified bowtie structure of the web [Broder et al., 2000].

A page p in IN has $ID(p) = 0$ and $OD(p) > 0$, such that it cannot be found by following links. Pages in OUT have $OD(p) = 0$ (except for links to pages in a TENDRIL, cf. below) and an $ID(p) > 0$, such that they can be found by following links, but, in fact, constitute a dead end. The strongly connected component (SCC) contains only pages with both $ID(p) > 0$ and $OD(p) > 0$, and it is the case that for any pages p_1 and p_2 within SCC, there is a link path from p_1 to p_2. A TENDRIL is either a page or a chain of linked pages which is linked to by a page from IN or OUT which does not lead to the SCC. A TUBE, which also can be a single page or a chain of pages, connects IN and OUT without offering a path to any of the SCC pages.

In Broder et al. [2000], it was found that the components have roughly equal sizes. The considerable size of IN, for example, is due to the fact that any freshly created page is usually not linked to by any other page at the moment of its creation. Typical pages in OUT are company websites, which often do not link to external pages. A more detailed and recent paper about the size of the components is Serrano et al. [2007]. The next section deals with general accessibility properties of web pages which lie beyond the question of whether they can be reached by following links.

2.2.2   ACCESSIBILITY AND STABILITY OF WEB PAGES

Crawling relies on the links between web pages to discover huge numbers of them, simply by recursively following some or all links from the downloaded pages. For this to work, the crawling process obviously needs to be started with a set of start URLs (the seeds) from which the discovery process begins. This section discusses which types of pages a crawler can retrieve, given this basic strategy.

A page p that has $ID(p) = 0$ cannot be retrieved by crawling unless its URL is known at the start. However, there are pages which cannot be retrieved for other reasons, even if their URLs are known. For example, a company web server might only serve documents to IP addresses which belong to the company. If the crawler is run from outside the company, it will not be able to download such content. Also, many web servers require login information to access all or some of the content provided (paid services, social networks, forums, etc.).

Even if no login is required, certain content is only served after a form has been filled out. The scripts which process the form input usually make sure that the input makes sense, i. e., that it was entered by a human and not guessed by a machine. Of course, even without such checks, the output generated by a form might be empty if the input is nonsensical. If a machine enters random words into the query field of a database front end which looks up information about medical drugs, for example, the output will most likely be empty in most cases. Such documents have to be considered part of the so-called *Deep Web*, which cannot be accessed without significant additional overhead compared to simple crawling. Search engine companies use advanced guessing strategies on web pages containing forms in order to surface otherwise hidden database content. Such techniques are beyond the scope of this book, but for further reading, Madhavan et al. [2009] is recommended.

Also, server administrators can ask crawling software to stay away from certain documents using the Robots Exclusion standard by creating a file *robots.txt* directly in the root directory of the server. The file contains information for (all or specific) crawlers as to which directories and documents they may retrieve, and which ones they must not retrieve. Pages blocked by Robots Exclusion are not technically part of the Deep Web, but are nevertheless inaccessible for web corpus construction. As will be explained in Section 2.3.3, not obeying a server's Robots Exclusion requests is unwise and can lead to a crawling institution acquiring a bad reputation. In the worst case, server administrators might block access by the crawler at the IP level.

Furthermore, a distinction must be made between a web URL and the document which can be retrieved by requesting the URL. Even traditional static pages are updated sporadically or periodically, i. e., old content is deleted or altered, and new content is added. Thus, a URL is never an appropriate identifier to address the contents of a single document. With the introduction of content-management systems, which generate pages from content databases each time the page is accessed (using HTTP header information or IP-based client geo-location to generate an appropriate page), this is now more true than ever. Not even two exactly synchronous accesses to a web page necessarily lead to the same document.

Finally, links are ephemeral, a property known as link rot. A URL which points to a document is never guaranteed to point to anything in the future. Link rot was studied from the early days of the development of the web. Seminal papers include Fetterly et al. [2003] and Bar-Yossef et al. [2004].

2.2.3 WHAT'S IN A (NATIONAL) TOP LEVEL DOMAIN?

In this section, we briefly discuss what levels of structure (strata) are usually assumed to be discernible within the whole web. We focus especially on (national) top level domains (*TLD*), because they play a major role in web corpus construction. Thus, with this section, we begin to consider the web as the population of documents from which we draw a sample when we build a static web corpus. The stratification of the final corpus depends on the stratification of the population (this section) and on our method of sampling (Sections 2.3 and 2.4).

Firstly, we can examine the more or less technical stratification of the web, as it is done in so-called web characterization. Technical features examined in web characterization include, e. g., URL lengths, quantities of different image formats, server software, link structure. A large-scale comparison of features, methods, and results (for 24 different countries) can be found in Baeza-Yates et al. [2007]. Put in a larger context, such features can be correlated with external features, as it is done in so-called Webometrics. A seminal paper on Webometrics, the quantitative study of the structure of the web in relation to social, economical, political, and other external variables, was Björneborn and Ingwersen [2004]. For an introductory text, cf. Thelwall [2009].

Björneborn and Ingwersen [2004] and the subsequent literature suggest that there are around ten levels of granularity in web characterization, and we reproduce here the diagram from Baeza-Yates et al. [2007, 3] in Figure 2.2.

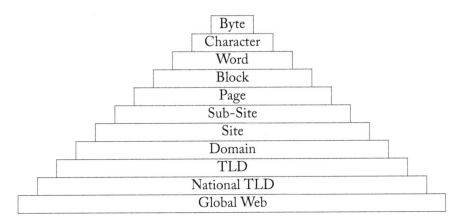

Figure 2.2: Web characterization: levels of granularity.

While the byte level is only relevant technically and in relation to the character level (e. g., in cases where one byte does not necessarily correspond to one character, cf. Section 3.2.3), the character level is of some importance for web corpus construction. This is because language identification (Section 3.4) is often based on the distribution of characters or character n-grams in documents. The word level can also be used in language identification, but additionally, words and blocks are also important in register and genre classification (not covered in this book).

The sub-site, site (roughly equivalent to host) and domain (roughly equivalent to server) levels provide important clues as to the nature of the sample of documents. If, for example, our web corpus is supposed to be a sample from a TLD, then for determining the success of the sampling process, it is crucial to check whether the distribution of hosts within the TLD fits the distribution of hosts in the corpus.

Finally, TLDs and national TLDs are important because many monolingual web corpora are based on crawls of national TLDs which belong to a country with a single dominant national language as a crude method of building monolingual corpora. This is true, e. g., for the WaCky corpora [Baroni et al., 2009] and the COW corpora [Schäfer and Bildhauer, 2012]. Also, many comparatively easy-to-calculate metrics have been studied for national TLDs. In Baeza-Yates et al. [2007], a greater number of studies of national TLDs were aggregated, and the authors found that most metrics have characteristic and stable distributions across all national TLDs (Figure 2.3). Almost all metrics are distributed according to a power law, and the α parameter can be estimated (cf. also Section 2.2.1). Such known metrics could and often should be used in adjusting the sampling procedure and in the evaluation of final corpora.[4,5,6]

In Figure 2.3, nothing is said about the distribution of languages. This is because the situation is different for every TLD. In cases where there is only one or one clearly dominant national language, the majority of pages not in this language is usually in English. In African countries, English pages are reported to account for over 75% of all pages, in Spain for 30%, and for 8% in Chile. For multilingual countries, statistics vary according to the individual socio-linguistic situation.

Since it was said above that crawling national TLDs is a *crude* method of constructing monolingual corpora, some consideration should be given to the question of how crude this method actually is. First of all, for countries with more than one dominant language or dialect, additional language identification and filtering is required. Secondly, the method does not work equally well for all national TLDs, especially when this TLD does not have high prestige. The .us TLD is a well-known example of a TLD with low prestige. If we crawled the .us domain, the yield of the crawl might be comparatively poor (considering the size of the U. S. English web), and certain types of documents might be underrepresented in the sample, simply because major organizations never use the .us TLD. The .es TLD is a good example of a mix of such problems. Among the official languages are three closely related ones (Castilian, Catalan, and Galician), which are all in use, even in online newspapers and on official websites. On the other

---

[4]In the Double Pareto cases, two α values are fitted. For example, file sizes are reported to follow a power law for smaller files, and another power law for larger files.

[5]Values for within-site links are normalized relative to the number of documents within the respective site.

[6]Basic data, including metrics for (national) TLDs, can be obtained from the survey regularly conducted by the Internet Systems Consortium: http://www.isc.org/solutions/survey/

Metric	Distribution	Parameter and mean examples for TLDs
file sizes in KB	Double Pareto	Korea: $\bar{x} = 10$, $\alpha_1 = 0.4$, $\alpha_2 = 3.7$ Brazil: $\bar{x} = 21$, $\alpha_1 = 0.3$, $\alpha_2 = 3.4$
page age in months	Exponential	Brazil: $\bar{x} = 11.6$, $\lambda = 2.1$ (rate) Greece: $\bar{x} = 17.7$, $\lambda = 1.6$ (rate)
pages per site	Pareto	Spain: $\bar{x} = 52$, $\alpha = 1.1$ Italy: $\bar{x} = 410$, $\alpha = 1.3$
sites per domain	Pareto	U. K.: $\bar{x} = 1.2$, $\alpha = 1.6$ Spain: $\bar{x} = 2.5$, $\alpha = 2.3$
in-degree	Pareto	Chile: $\bar{x} = 8.3$, $\alpha = 2.0$ U. K.: $\bar{x} = 16.2$, $\alpha = 1.8$
out-degree	Double Pareto	Spain: $\bar{x} = 3.6$, $\alpha_1 = 0.9$, $\alpha_2 = 4.2$ Italy: $\bar{x} = 31.9$, $\alpha_1 = 0.7$, $\alpha_2 = 2.5$
average within-site links	Double Pareto	Spain: $\bar{x} = 0.1$, $\alpha_1 = 1.5$, $\alpha_2 = 2.5$ Brazil: $\bar{x} = 3.5$, $\alpha_1 = 0.8$, $\alpha_2 = 2.9$
URL length (characters)	Log-Normal	Portugal: $\bar{x} = 67$ U. K.: $\bar{x} = 76$

Figure 2.3: Examples of web characterization metrics [Baeza-Yates et al., 2007] with illustrative examples. Countries were chosen here to illustrate the typical range of values as found in the aforementioned paper.

hand, the .es domain does have a mixed prestige in Spain. While the largest Spanish newspaper El País prefers the non-national domain elpais.com, the second largest newspaper El Mundo uses the national domain elmundo.es.

Another question goes beyond the problems just outlined, namely whether national TLDs of different countries actually represent national variants. Cook and Hirst [2012] recently found that for .ca and .uk, features of Canadian and U. K. English can actually be detected in corpora compiled from national TLD crawls. The method they use is based on comparisons to traditionally compiled corpora of the respective varieties, applying both keyword comparison (Kilgarriff, 2009; see also Section 5.4) and comparison of spelling variants. Such tendencies, however, are only observable for entire corpora, and they do not warrant the conclusion that any specific document downloaded from the .uk domain can be safely assumed to represent U. K. English. In fact, the known similarity of a U. K. web corpus to a traditional corpus of U. K. English like the BNC [Leech, 1993] with respect to keyword distributions does not necessarily allow us to draw any further conclusions, for example that the syntax of the web corpus bears a significant resemblance to the traditional corpus. It is an open question whether linguists could and should do research on regional variants of languages using crawls of national TLDs.[7]

2.2.4   PROBLEMATIC SEGMENTS OF THE WEB

In this section, we briefly discuss two kinds of segments of the web that are most likely unattractive for corpus construction. We also discuss how they can be avoided, leading over to Section 2.3.

First, with the advent of content management systems and other kinds of content generated ad hoc by scripts executed on web servers, in most cases using underlying data bases (generally called *dynamic web pages*), many websites are of virtually infinite size. The standard example cited in many papers is a script-based calendar system which generates links from any day, month, or year view to the subsequent view of the same kind. The virtually infinite segments of the web, which are generated by such systems, can be detected relatively easily because:

1. all links are host-internal,
2. the link URLs contain HTTP GET parameters (after the ?).

This means that such link sequences can be avoided by:

1. setting a quota on the maximum number of pages per host or per server allowed in our sample,
2. stripping all GET parameters from link URLs, or
3. keeping track of and limiting the depth of a link chain a crawler follows within a single host.

Techniques 1 and 2 are problematic because they will inevitably lead to many pages being excluded that are not part of the kind of web graph segment which we are trying to ignore. Especially host and server quotas might lead to many pages being excluded from the sample. As it was shown in Figure 2.3, the pages per site and sites per domain metrics follow a Pareto distribution. Strongly represented hosts (forum and blog providers like *Blogspot* or *Wordpress* or newspapers) would most likely not be represented adequately in the sample. Technique 3 is therefore preferable.

The second kind of problematic segment is more difficult to detect, mostly because it is created with the intention of being hard to detect. Search engines use not only the contents of web documents to determine whether the document is relevant to a specific user query, but they also weight the results by the link context a page stands in. Simply speaking, the higher the in-degree of a page, the higher its relevance (cf. Section 2.4.2 for a brief introduction to the more adequate PageRank metric). This strategy is used and/or abused by content providers to improve their position in search engine rankings. A bundle of techniques called search engine

---

[7]In 2013, Mark Davies released a corpus of English web documents classified according to Google geo-location information. No scientific papers have been released describing or evaluating the quality of this resource, but it might be an interesting project in the context of the questions discussed in this section: http://corpus2.byu.edu/glowbe/

optimization (SEO) is used, one of the most popular being link farm creation. A link farm is a number of servers or hosts which serve documents with very high link degrees among them. This heightens the reputation of the pages in search engines, such that links from the link farm to, e. g., product listings or commercial services also acquire a high reputation.

Link farms are not as easy to detect as are virtually infinite (but benevolent) websites, because:

1. they are distributed between different hosts,
2. they often serve fake content, either auto-generated or obtained by scraping content from other websites,
3. there are other benevolent communities with similar link structures (e. g., the so-called blogosphere).

Techniques to avoid the sampling of link farms are beyond the scope of this book. The number of papers dedicated to SEO and counter-measures by search engines is huge, but a recommended introduction to this whole field of adversarial web search is Castillo and Davison [2011]. Some available crawlers (to be discussed immediately in Section 2.3) implement at least some techniques to avoid link farms, or they can be extended to implement such techniques.

2.3   CRAWLING BASICS

2.3.1   INTRODUCTION

Crawling (sometimes also called spidering, with minimal semantic differences) is the recursive process of discovering and downloading web pages by following links extracted (or *harvested*) from pages already known. In its simplest form, crawling is a breadth-first traversal of the web graph by extracting all URLs from all downloaded pages and adding them to one huge queue of URLs of pages yet to be downloaded. At least under the assumption that the web is static, and given the macroscopic structure of the web as described in Section 2.2.1, one start URL from the IN or SCC component is enough to start a discovery process which will eventually lead to the discovery of the whole SCC. This is because we required that for each pair of pages p_1 and p_2 in SCC, there must be a link path from p_1 to p_2. In theory, it is also possible to do an exhaustive Random Walk through the web graph, if we have enough crawling time and a backtrack mechanism to return from accidentally crawled pages in OUT or a TENDRIL. In a Random Walk, the software follows a randomly selected single link from each page without queueing the other links. More on Random Walks can be found in Section 2.4.

Of course, the web is not static (although, pragmatically, for many experiments such an assumption is made), because it contains potential infinities, and it is extremely large. Therefore, exhaustive crawls are practically impossible.[8] The immense size of the web means that a web

---

[8]Notice that infinite paths such as described in Section 2.2.4 are not necessarily a TENDRIL. Taking up the calendar example, each auto-generated page might also contain links back to normal SCC pages, such that the infinite path is fully contained in SCC.

corpus will always be a rather small sample from it. Even in 2005, the indexable web (roughly the web without the Deep Web and virtual infinities) was estimated at 11.5 billion pages by Gulli and Signorini [2005], and in July 2008, Jesse Alpert and Nissan Hajaj of Google announced in an official blog post that they had indexed the significantly larger number of one trillion web pages.[9] The art of efficient crawling therefore consists in finding the most relevant pages as early as possible during the crawl. This is usually formulated as the task of maximizing the weighted coverage WC of a crawl at each crawl time t, where $C(t)$ is the set of crawled pages at t and w a weight function, which determines the relevance of each page relative to the goal of the crawl [Olston and Najork, 2010, 29]:

$$WC(t) = \sum_{p \in C(t)} w(p) \qquad (2.2)$$

The definition of w is crucial in determining strategies for the optimization of the weighted coverage. As will be discussed in Section 2.4, available crawling strategies are often well understood under a search engine (SE) perspective, where the weight function w_{SE} is such that, for example, pages with a high in-degree (or rather a high PageRank, cf. Section 2.4.2) are assigned a high weight. However, if we are looking for pages which might not necessarily be popular or authoritative in a search engine sense, strategies have to be adapted.

Before going into such details, however, we first need to clarify the practical steps which are identical for virtually all crawling strategies. These are:

1. Collect a set of URLs to start with (usually called *seed URLs* or just *seeds*),
2. configure the crawler software to accept only desired content (TLD restrictions, file name patterns, MIME types, file sizes, languages and encodings, etc.),
3. decide on crawler politeness settings, i. e., the settings which influence the strain the crawler puts on any of the hosts from which it tries to retrieve documents (the number of requests within a certain period of time, the bandwidth, etc.),
4. run the crawler, usually observing its progress to make sure the crawl does not "go wrong."

Since a popular implementation of step 1 is identical to a simpler and crawling-free method of web corpus construction—the BootCaT method—we first describe this method now in Section 2.3.2.

2.3.2   CORPUS CONSTRUCTION FROM SEARCH ENGINE RESULTS

In this section, we describe the BootCaT method of web corpus construction, mainly because its first step can also be used as a method to gather seed URLs, and because it played a historic role in practical ad-hoc web corpus construction. It was described in Baroni and Bernardini [2004] and is implemented as a chain of shell scripts plus a Java-based GUI called BootCaT ("Boot-

---

[9]http://googleblog.blogspot.de/2008/07/we-knew-web-was-big.html

strapping Corpora And Terms from the Web").[10] The goal is to obtain random samples from a search engine's index (possibly restricted to URLs from one national TLD), download the pages corresponding to the returned URLs, and create a corpus from them. The corpora are relatively small compared to crawled corpora, but the method itself and its implementation are quite user-friendly, minimizing the effort that needs to be invested in the construction of the corpus.

As it was described in Chapter 1, search engine query results are not uniform random samples from the search engine's index, but the exact opposite, namely samples which are extremely biased toward documents which the search engine provider has classified as relevant according to some metric unknown to the user. For entirely different purposes, namely the comparative benchmarking of search engine performance and coverage, researchers have tried to figure out ways of sampling randomly from search engines' indexes without having direct access to the database. This kind of research starts with Bharat and Broder [1998]; an important later paper was Bar-Yossef and Gurevich [2006], which also summarizes the criticism of the method proposed by Bharat and Broder.

In Bharat and Broder [1998], it is suggested to

1. construct a lexicon of terms with their frequencies as found on the web,
2. eliminate extremely low frequency terms (which might be misspellings or other types of noisy tokens as discussed in Chapter 4),
3. formulate random multi-word queries (both conjunctions and disjunctions) by sampling words from the lexicon according to their frequency,
4. pick URLs from the set of URLs returned by the search engine uniformly at random.

There is no restriction to using query words in a specific language in this proposal. As Bharat and Broder notice, there are a number of biases which this method introduces. There is a ranking bias, because for most queries, the search engine could return many more results than it actually does. Only the results which are considered to be the most relevant are actually returned by the search engine, which makes true uniform random sampling from the results impossible.

The second most important bias is the query bias. By sending very specific combinations of terms, we ask for longer, content-rich pages, because they have a higher chance of matching such queries. In the worst case (also mentioned in Bar-Yossef and Gurevich, 2006), many results are dictionaries or word lists. To illustrate these theoretical findings, Figure 2.4 shows the result of one of our own experiments from May 2012. We queried a meta-search engine with 10,000 unique 4-tuples constructed from 5,000 mid-frequency Celex [Baayen et al., 1995] word forms (rank 1,001–6,000). 127,910 URLs were harvested; 70,897 of them were unique (55.43%). The figure shows the top 15 returned pages and how often they were returned. It is immediately obvious that querying random 4-tuples very often leads to documents which are word lists and similar resources.

---

[10]http://bootcat.sslmit.unibo.it/

Count	URL
3947	http://www.let.rug.nl/~vannoord/ftp/DutchBrillTagging/Entire_Corpus/BIGWORDLIST
2768	http://www.ai.rug.nl/vakinformatie/PTenS/pract/docs/totrank.txt
2682	http://hmi.ewi.utwente.nl/spraakgroep/capita[…]bn-baseline.until310806.51K.v2.vocab
2022	http://www.ntg.nl/spelling/latin1/woorden.min
1293	http://www.ntg.nl/spelling/latin1/woorden.med
1088	http://anw.inl.nl/doc/lemmalijst%2015%20plus.txt
1021	http://anw.inl.nl/doc/fulllemmalist.txt
959	http://www.ekudos.nl/artikel/nieuw?url=$href&title=$title&desc=$lead
948	http://homepages.cwi.nl/~jve/lexsem/Lemma_Pos_Frq_CGN.lst
762	http://www.ntg.nl/spelling/ibmpc437/woorden.min
650	http://www.win.tue.nl/~keesh/dokuwiki/lib/exe/fetch.php?[…]dutchwords.txt
603	https://www.os3.nl/_media/2008-2009/students/willem_toorop/woorden.txt
591	http://www.ai.rug.nl/nl/vakinformatie/PTenS/pract/docs/totrank.txt
534	http://ens.ewi.tudelft.nl/donau/groene_boekje
364	http://www.let.rug.nl/~vannoord/ftp/DutchBrillTagging/Entire_Corpus/BIGBIGRAMLIST
343	http://frii.nl/outfile.txt
331	https://www.os3.nl/_media/2008-2009/[…]/ssn/practicum/opdracht_2/dutch.txt
313	http://www.ai.rug.nl/vakinformatie/PTenS/docs/totrank.txt
309	http://www.ntg.nl/spelling/ibmpc437/woorden.med
275	http://www.let.rug.nl/~vannoord/ftp/DutchBrillTagging/Entire_Corpus/TRAINING.LEXICON

Figure 2.4: Top pages returned for random 4-tuples (Dutch Celex word list) sent to a meta-search engine with the number of times they were returned. Very long lines are abbreviated by [...].

To alleviate biases, Bar-Yossef and Gurevich suggest and evaluate Monte Carlo methods of random sampling under difficult sampling conditions, such as the Metropolis-Hastings algorithm. They also modify the sampling procedure, effectively performing a Random Walk through the search engines' indexes. For the BootCaT method, however, the assumption is that sending 3- or 4-tuples of mid-frequency terms as conjunct queries to search engines and harvesting the first n results is a random enough process or at least that it delivers documents which are relevant and diverse enough for corpus construction [Ciaramita and Baroni, 2006]. It has to be kept in mind, however, that the returned documents will at least be biased toward word lists and long documents. Whether a corpus designer is satisfied with this is an individual decision.

We also have to keep in mind the facts mentioned in Chapter 1 about implicit search term modification. Whether or not they are a result of sponsored ranking, search results for random tuples as in Figure 2.5 are common. Notice the morphological modification of search terms (*glory* for *glorious*) and even the expansion of lexical words to brand names (*circles* to *PureCircle*). This, above all, means that controlling the frequencies of the words used for the construction of the queries is quite ineffective, because the search engine heavily modifies the queries. See Chapter 1 (esp. page 2) for further search term modifications applied by search engines.

One final practical problem makes the BootCaT method unattractive. To construct corpora of considerable size, a lot of queries need to be sent to the search engine in an automated way. Search engines usually do not allow this both legally and technically. API-based access for bulk requests used to be available during beta phases of all major search engine providers, but the last

Query: `glorious discretion virtually unhappy`

Dancing in the Glory of Monsters Jason Stearns[1]
Dancing in the **Glory** of Monsters Jason Stearns[1] - Free ebook download as ...and could
legislate by decree and change the constitution at his **discretion**. ...a fanciful spiritual
order that sold banking licenses in the name of a **virtual** state. ...was hospitalized in South
Africa—and was obviously **unhappy** with the question.
www.scribd.com/.../Dancing-in-the-Glory-of-... – Cachad

Query: `circles texts ingredients procurement`

PureCircle: high purity stevia volumes up 20% plus
9 Jul 2012 ...Carbohydrates and fibres (sugar, starches) · Cereals and bakery preparations ·
Chocolate and confectionery **ingredients** · Cultures, enzymes, yeast ...**Text** size Print Email
...High purity stevia volume sales at **PureCircle** have increased by ...kindly send me details
of **procuring** good quality stevia extract in ...
www.foodnavigator.com/.../PureCircle-High-p... – Cachad

Figure 2.5: Top-ranked Google results for some random English tuples on July 31, 2012, queried using a Swedish Firefox from a German IP. The output is a verbatim reproduction of the entries in the Google results page, including the document summary.

free API by a major provider (Microsoft Bing) was shut down in late 2012. Major providers like Bing, Google, and Yahoo also do not serve clients like `curl` or `GNU wget`, which could be abused to send huge amounts of requests without an API, extracting the results from the normal HTML pages returned.[11,12] Finally, even if someone manages to send bulk queries, her/his IP addresses usually get banned very quickly. Thus, the BootCaT method can no longer be used productively, unless the user is willing to pay and capable of paying significant amounts of money for search engine API access. It can be test-run, however, using the BootCaT tools and very limited demo access. These problems with the BootCaT method have consequences for crawling approaches, as will become clear in Section 2.3.5.

2.3.3   CRAWLERS AND CRAWLER PERFORMANCE

We now turn to the basic architecture of crawler software with a focus on those configurable parts of the software which influence the performance. A crawler (also: bot, robot, spider) is a piece of software that performs the act of crawling as defined in Section 2.3.1. Starting from a set of URLs (seeds), it proceeds to discover virtually unlimited amounts of pages by following links. Using a crawler, as opposed to BootCaT-like tools, therefore allows the construction of corpora

---

[11]http://curl.haxx.se/
[12]http://www.gnu.org/software/wget

virtually unlimited in size. For example, Pomikálek et al. [2012] describe a 70 Billion word corpus of English based on the 1 Billion page ClueWeb09 data set,[13] which was obtained via crawling.

Crawler architectures are conceptually rather simple, but require careful implementations if the crawler is intended to sustain a high download rate over long crawl times. To give an approximation of the rate at which the crawler must download documents, we first need to get an impression of how many of the downloaded documents will make it into the corpus. Of course, this rate of loss due to cleanups depends on many design decisions, i. e., on the definition of which documents should be removed. Table 2.6 gives the figures for the DECOW2012 corpus [Schäfer and Bildhauer, 2012]. The cleanup steps correspond roughly to what will be described in Chapter 3.

Algorithm removes...	No. of documents	Percentage
very short pages	93,604,922	71.67%
non-text documents	16,882,377	12.93%
perfect duplicates	3,179,884	2.43%
near-duplicates	9,175,335	7.03%
total	122,842,518	94.06%

Figure 2.6: Amount of documents lost in the cleanup steps of DECOW2012, a 9 billion token corpus of German from a crawl of the .de domain.

Over 90% of the documents (in this case 94.06%) do not make it into the final corpus. Let us assume for the sake of simplicity that we could keep 10% of the documents. This means that we have to crawl at least ten times as many documents as we actually require. For a one million document corpus, we would have to crawl 27.8 hours at a rate of 100 documents per second. If we only achieve half that speed, crawling time will be 55.5 hours, etc.

For each document, the crawler has to perform DNS lookups, possibly wait for a few seconds due to politeness reasons (Section 2.3.4), send the HTTP request, wait for the response, maybe retry, and finally extract the links from the retrieved documents. Therefore, a reasonably high download rate can only be achieved by a multi-threaded program or a fully parallelized piece of software which is capable of running on a cluster of machines. This, however, increases the complexity of the whole system, since the huge data structures which we will describe in the next paragraphs need to be synchronized between the different machines.

An introduction to crawler design is Chapter 20 of Manning et al. [2009]. Here, we only list the most important components that a crawler user minimally has to be aware of, ignoring implementation and parallelization issues completely. A crawler consists of the following components (not mentioning those which are less critical in configuration, like the file writer which stores the downloaded content):

---

[13]http://lemurproject.org/clueweb09/

- **fetcher**—a massively multi-threaded component which downloads documents corresponding to URLs in the **frontier**,
- **parser** or **harvester**—a component which extracts new URLs from web pages (at least from `<a href></a>` tags),
- **URL filters**—code that discards URLs which are duplicate or which do not conform to certain criteria (length, blacklisted hosts, Robots Exclusion, etc.),
- **frontier**—data structures which store, queue, and prioritize URLs and finally pass them to the fetcher.

Crawlers can slow down because of huge data structures in the frontier which grow over time, and because the fetcher usually spends a lot of time just waiting. To illustrate frontier growth, assume a frontier contains 100 million URLs and a URL is a string of a mean length of 64 bytes (which is roughly adequate, cf. Figure 2.3 on page 13). This produces approximately 5.96 GB of data just for the URLs in the frontier. Such amounts of data can be processed in memory today, but if we want to calculate with even simple weight functions (cf. Section 2.3.1) in order to re-prioritize such a large queue, we will lose a lot of time. To make a crawler scale arbitrarily, we cannot even rely on there being enough system memory, however, and disk-based re-prioritization of such huge queues takes considerably longer.

Even the URL filters create large data structures, for example if a URL Seen Test is used. A URL Seen Test determines for any harvested URL whether it was already downloaded or is already queued to avoid multiple queuing of the same URL. Performing a naïve database lookup would be far too slow, so usually Bloom filters or similar algorithms are used.[14] Classic Bloom filters require approximately m bits for a set S with $n = |S|$ and ϵ the desired probability of a false positive [Broder and Mitzenmacher, 2004, 491]:

$$m \geq n \frac{\log_2(\frac{1}{\epsilon})}{\ln 2} \tag{2.3}$$

For example, assuming $|S| = 10^8$ and a false positive rate of one every 1^5 keys on average ($\epsilon = 10^{-5}$), we require at least 91.17 MB of RAM. This is not a huge amount of RAM by today's standards, but if we go up to $|S| = 10^9$, we are already at 911.69 MB, etc. To make the software scale arbitrarily, such (and much worse) scenarios have to be considered.[15]

As mentioned before, the second bottleneck during the runtime of a crawler is the long idle (i. e., waiting) time during or in-between requests. First of all, DNS lookups (the process of

---

[14]A Bloom filter as proposed in Bloom [1970] is an efficient set membership detection algorithm with no chance of false negatives and a known chance of false positives. Bloom filters do not store the keys themselves, but store a single long bit array A of a length l (proportional to the desired error rate), with all bits initially unset. To add a key, the key is hashed with n hash functions which produce values $a_i \in [1..l]$. For each added key and each of its corresponding hash values $a_i, i \in [1..n]$, the bit at $A[a_i]$ is set. To check for set membership, one checks whether the bits at all $A[a_i]$ are set. To avoid false negatives, it is not allowed to remove values from the set, i. e., bits cannot be unset. A good introduction to and survey of Bloom filters is Broder and Mitzenmacher [2004].

[15]Space-optimized variants of the Bloom filter as discussed for example in Pagh et al. [2005] usually come with a time penalty and vice-versa.

requesting an IP address for a host name) take up time, such that DNS information for recently encountered hosts should be cached. Additional activity and waiting time is incurred by politeness conventions (cf. Section 2.3.4). When the fetcher finally requests the document, it goes to sleep, possibly for seconds, just waiting for the data to arrive. Extracting the links, however, can then be done effectively by regular expression matching (i. e., not necessarily using a DOM parse, cf. Section 3.2.1), and does not bring about many performance problems. Given these delays, the crawler can only achieve reasonable performance when it is massively parallel. Parallelization in this case does not necessarily mean that a lot of processing power is needed: The threads/processes will be in a sleeping/waiting state most of the time.

Finally, it should be mentioned that the calculation of the crawl rate on page 20 was naïve in one important way. The crawler can guess (by simple regular expression matching) that certain types of URLs are definitely not of the desired type. Usually, URLs ending in `.jpg` or `.flv` etc. can be safely assumed to lead to binary non-text multimedia content. However, many URLs do not clearly signal the type of data which is served when they are requested, for example if the default page from a directory is called (URL ends in /), or when a server script is called (file part of the URL ends in `.php`, `.asp`, etc., possibly followed by GET parameters after the ?). The crawler has to download such content but has to dispose of it immediately, just by looking at the MIME type of the received data (which is only known after successful download). It could be configured to keep only `text/html` and `text/xml` for example. Since the calculation of the download rate was based only on the original amount of HTML data that was actually stored by the crawler, we need to discover and download even more documents. It is also wise to set a maximum file size, instructing the crawler to stop downloading a file larger than a few hundred KB. This is because such large files are most likely binary/multimedia files. Without a size limit, we also regularly crawled documents over 1 GB large which were in fact HTML documents generated by faulty server scripts stuck in a loop, emitting the same error message until some server or crawler timeout was reached. Table 2.8 (at the end of Section 2.3.4) summarizes all important performance-critical features of a crawler mentioned so far.

Available industry-strength and free crawler products include `Heritrix` [Mohr et al., 2004].[16] It is relatively easy to configure, offers robust single-machine parallelization, but is not well suited to be run on a cluster of machines. A crawler which is capable of running on clusters of machines (but can of course also run on a single machine) is `Nutch`.[17] The overhead of setting up a cluster both in terms of work time and in terms of parallelization overhead should be carefully balanced against the expected gain in scalability, however. In our experience, crawling in the region of a few 10^8 documents does not require setting up a cluster. If the `Java` VM is given at least 5 GB of RAM, and the crawler stores its data files on fast machine-local hard drives (not NFS storage or other slow file systems), then such a crawl can be completed within days or maximally a few weeks, using a pool of 100 to 200 threads.

---

[16]`http://webarchive.jira.com/wiki/display/Heritrix`
[17]`http://nutch.apache.org/`

2.3.4   CONFIGURATION DETAILS AND POLITENESS

It was already mentioned in Section 2.3.3 that there should be some criteria by which the crawler discards documents during and after download. However, some simple filters can also be applied to the harvested URLs before they are even queued, avoiding some of the overhead of documents which are crawled but later discarded. This section briefly mentions these filters as well as the necessary politeness settings any crawler should implement.

Among the filter criteria applied to URLs are restrictions to a certain domain, either at the TLD level or at the server level. If we want to compile a corpus of online newspaper text, we might want to restrict the servers to be crawled to those of the ten or twenty most important newspaper servers, for example. URL-based scope restrictions are like a whitelist, which explicitly instructs the crawler what to crawl.

On the other hand, the crawler should be capable of handling IP and URL blacklists. For a variety of purposes (e. g., ad filtering in browsers), there are block lists available, listing IPs or server names of spam or ad servers, for example. If the crawler just discards URLs which match an entry from such a list, it can save a significant amount of time. The same might be true if the user has identified link farms or simply keywords which occur in certain types of URLs leading to websites which do not serve documents containing much usable text (like porn sites, gambling sites, etc.).

URLs are also usually canonicalized. This minimally involves lowercasing them, since URLs are not case-sensitive, and we can thus eliminate spurious duplicates. It is also possible to remove `https` URLs or alter them to `http`, because a secure protocol is not needed since no actual personal data is transmitted. Along the same lines, login information as in `http://user:pass@server` should be removed, and if desired, even GET parameters after the ? can be purged. If not purged, they should at least be sorted alphabetically to avoid URLs which point to the same content, but which contain the same parameters in a different order. For example, the following GET parameter specifications are equivalent: `?p1=v1&p2=v2` and `?p2=v2&p1=v1`.

Session IDs in GET parameters can always be safely removed. They are IDs in the form of hash strings by which a server can identify a user who interacts with the server over a span of time (the session). The server uses the ID to identify stored information about a user over successive requests made by this user, e. g., a shopping basket, viewing preferences, form data entered in previous steps, and even login credentials, provided the user passes the correct session ID with each request. Among the many ways of transmitting a session ID is adding them to the GET parameters, where different server scripting languages sometimes prefix their own name to the name of the parameter (`JSESSIONID` for Java, `PHPSESSID` for PHP, etc.). The most important reason to remove them is that they might create a lot of unique URLs pointing to the same content, and that the URL Seen Test will classify all of them as unseen.

As for the politeness, there are common recommendations and the Robots Exclusion standard. The common recommendations concern the frequency with which the crawler sends requests to a single host. First of all, most crawlers make sure that there are not two threads which request documents from the same server (IP) at the same time. Additionally, the crawler should wait several seconds (at least three, better five) before re-requesting the same page after a time-out or before requesting another page from the same server. It is therefore necessary to cache the information about which servers have been sent a request recently.

Robots Exclusion allows the web server administrator to explicitly ask all crawlers or a specific crawler to obey certain restrictions via the *robots.txt* file. It should be noticed that the Robots Exclusion standard is not an official standard, but rather a de facto standard with slightly varying interpretations by different crawlers.

To make Robots Exclusion work, a crawler must identify itself by a stable identifier via the User-Agent header sent in HTTP requests. The identifier contains a name (Googlebot for Google's crawler) and optionally information about the crawler, for example a URL which leads administrators to a website containing information about the purpose of the crawl. It is almost inevitable that crawler operators receive occasional complaints by server administrators, and in such cases it is helpful if the operator can rightfully claim that all standard politeness conventions were obeyed. The header might look like this, for example:

```
berlin-fu-cow (+http://hpsg.fu-berlin.de/cow)
```

The identifier can be used by server administrators in the *robots.txt* to identify a section of instructions for this specific crawler, cf. Figure 2.7. The section contains a sequence of Allow and Disallow directives, which allow/disallow access to directories or files specified relative to the host where the robots file itself resides. The snippet in Figure 2.7 first disallows access to any file under the root directory, i. e., it denies access to everything. Then, there is an Allow directive which opens up the /archives/ path (and everything below it). The directives have to be interpreted sequentially, and for each concrete file, the last directive which applies determines the actual access rights. Also, the crawler is asked to wait 10 seconds in between requests to this host through the Crawl-delay directive.

```
berlin-fu-cow:
Disallow: /
Allow: /archives/
Crawl-delay: 10
```

Figure 2.7: Sample *robots.txt* entry.

Thus, before the crawler requests a page, or better before a URL is added to the queue in the first place, the *robots.txt* for the host must be parsed to check whether the crawler is allowed to download the URL in question. Consequently, Robots Exclusion information should also be cached, because it is a waste of bandwidth and time to fetch and parse the *robots.txt* each time in case multiple pages from the same host are downloaded.

Figure 2.8 summarizes important user-configurable and performance-critical features of a crawler mentioned in Section 2.3.3 and this section as well as their purpose. We now turn to the task of gathering seed URLs in Section 2.3.5.

Feature	Purpose
URL scope restriction	Focus the crawl on TLDs like .uk or (lists of) servers.
URL file pattern filters	Do not queue URLs which clearly lead to undesirable content.
URL canonicalization	Strip login information, session IDs, make lowercase to avoid spurious duplicates.
IP and URL blacklists	Avoid spam, link farms, ads, etc.
file size restrictions	Discard too small files after download and too large files while downloading.
MIME type filter	Discard undesirable file types after download.
fetcher thread pool size	Control the overall performance, especially the download rate.
general politeness delays	Be nice to servers if no *robots.txt* is specified.
configurable `User-Agent` header	Make crawler recognizable.

Figure 2.8: Summary of critical user-configurable features of a crawler and their purposes.

2.3.5   SEED URL GENERATION

In this section we look at the task of collecting seed URLs for the crawler to start the page discovery process described in Section 2.3.1. We assume that seeds in one specific language for monolingual corpus construction are required. Essentially, web corpus designers need to ask themselves the following questions:

1. How many seed URLs are required?
2. Does any notion of "quality" play a role in seed selection?
3. Do they have to be diverse, i. e., cover a lot of different hosts, documents from different genres, etc.?

As for question 1, the answer depends on what the corpus designer expects. As argued in Section 2.2.1, one start URL from SCC is enough to eventually locate all pages within SCC. If we start with one such page and harvest and queue each URL we discover, then we discover the whole SCC and OUT. However, it might be the case that certain seeds help to maximize the weighted coverage (*WC*) as defined in Section 2.3.1, so question 1 leads directly to question 2. Using a lot of seeds to maximize the *WC* only makes sense if they help to discover more relevant documents more quickly, making both questions unanswerable without a definition of a weight function w to determine the relevance of pages.[18] In an experiment in 2011, we defined a makeshift weight func-

---

[18]In connection with the crawling strategy/sampling method, a more fundamental question than *WC* maximization arises: Does the selection of seeds influence the chance of discovering relevant segments of the web graph? This question can only be answered against a significant background in graph sampling methods (cf. Section 2.4 for a minimal background). Maiya and Berger-Wolf, 2011, 110, present some recent results from comparable networks, showing that many common crawling strategies suffer from relatively high seed sensitivity.

tion (similar to Suchomel and Pomikálek, 2012): If the corpus post-processing chain (HTML removal, boilerplate removal, language/text detection, perfect duplicate removal) does not discard the document, its weight is 1, else it is 0. Usually [Baroni et al., 2009; Schäfer and Bildhauer, 2012], seed URLs collected using a procedure identical to the BootCaT method (Section 2.3.2) are considered high quality seeds, so we performed two relatively short crawls (amassing 400 GB of raw data each) of the .es domain, looking for Castilian documents. One was seeded with 231,484 seed URLs from search engine queries, one with 10 such seed URLs. Figure 2.9 plots the ratio of output data and input data for snapshots of 400 MB over the crawler runtime.

Figure 2.9 shows that the final output/input ratio is roughly the same for a crawl with many seeds and for a crawl with few seeds, both in terms of the number of files and the amount of data left over after post-processing. In the initial phase, however, the crawl started with many seeds clearly achieves a better *WC*. This is true for both the file count and the amount of data, and it goes on for some time after the seeds themselves are exhausted. With many seeds, the crawler obviously downloads longer documents, fewer non-text documents, and fewer duplicates in the initial phase, producing more output for the total amount of data downloaded. All this does not happen much faster (cf. $\Delta t_{1..500}$), but the drop in time efficiency, which is inevitable with every crawl, does not occur while crawling the first 400 GB: While $\Delta t_{501..1000}$ goes up to 35.73h with few seeds, it is still at 18.75h with many seeds.[19]

We see that seed URLs from search engine queries are biased toward long and content-rich documents with a high chance of being in the correct language (because of the conjunct tuple query method used to obtain them). We also see that in the breadth-first neighborhood of such documents, there are other similar documents. All in all, it appears as if the drop in crawler efficiency comes roughly 200 GB later according to this experiment. Clearly, the importance of the improved *WC* in the initial phase is debatable if the final amount of data crawled is in the area of 5 TB or higher. Keeping in mind that even the definition of the weight function used in the experiment is very debatable (because it says that, in essence, we want a corpus which is biased toward long documents), we can plausibly assume that a moderate amount of seeds is sufficient. In Section 2.4.3, we briefly describe focused crawling strategies which could sustain a high *WC* throughout the crawl. This is not (or only weakly) possible by selecting more or better seeds, but by adapting the algorithm by which the crawler selects and prioritizes the URLs to follow.

If we do not find a way of collecting any reasonable amount of seeds from search engines using the BootCaT method, there are still other options. If language-classified seeds are required, the Open Directory Project offers links to websites in diverse languages in the *World* category.[20] The full data can be downloaded as an RDF dump, and links are easily extracted. If the corpus designer is satisfied with newspaper seeds, directories like ABYZ New Links can be used.[21] Finally, Wikipedia dumps are available in many languages, and they usually contain many links to sites

---

[19]The crawlers were run on the same machine, with the same bandwidth and using the same NFS storage for crawler state, logs, and data. Both were run with 75 fetcher threads. The NFS storage explains for the overall suboptimal time performance.
[20]http://www.dmoz.org/
[21]http://abyznewslinks.com/

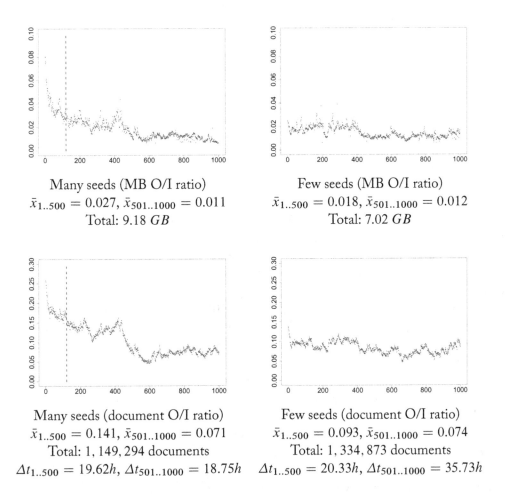

Many seeds (MB O/I ratio)
$\bar{x}_{1..500} = 0.027, \bar{x}_{501..1000} = 0.011$
Total: 9.18 GB

Few seeds (MB O/I ratio)
$\bar{x}_{1..500} = 0.018, \bar{x}_{501..1000} = 0.012$
Total: 7.02 GB

Many seeds (document O/I ratio)
$\bar{x}_{1..500} = 0.141, \bar{x}_{501..1000} = 0.071$
Total: 1, 149, 294 documents
$\Delta t_{1..500} = 19.62h, \Delta t_{501..1000} = 18.75h$

Few seeds (document O/I ratio)
$\bar{x}_{1..500} = 0.093, \bar{x}_{501..1000} = 0.074$
Total: 1, 334, 873 documents
$\Delta t_{1..500} = 20.33h, \Delta t_{501..1000} = 35.73h$

Figure 2.9: Comparison of the yield from breadth-first crawls in the .es TLD, started with (i) 231,484 and (ii) 10 Yahoo seed URLs. Castilian 4-tuples were queried. Crawled using `Heritrix` 1.14 in May and June 2011. The x-axis is the n-th archive file produced by the crawler (400 MB of uncompressed input data each). The y-axis is the output/input ratio for these archive files. The input underwent HTML-stripping, boilerplate removal, text detection based on high-frequency function words, and perfect duplicate detection. Means were calculated for the first and second half of the crawls. The vertical line marks the 120th archive, where the seed URLs were exhausted.

in these languages. Since a larger number of links in Wikipedia dumps leads to English websites, applying additional language identification for the seeds is advised (cf. Section 3.4).

One problem with crawling monolingual corpora which we have not discussed in detail so far is crawling for languages which cannot be associated with a (set of) national TLDs. Even if we find seeds in such languages, any random crawl will sooner or later deliver a majority of documents in other languages, significantly spoiling the *WC*. We will discuss a possible solution in Section 2.4.3.

2.4 MORE ON CRAWLING STRATEGIES

2.4.1 INTRODUCTION

So far, we have implicitly pretended that implementing the crawling process in software just requires a series of engineering decisions, for example dealing with implementation tasks such as the URL Seen Test, huge queues, multi-threading, etc. (all in Section 2.3.3). In this section, we examine some quite fundamental questions regarding crawling strategies. The discussion is most likely relevant for researchers (for example theoretical/empirical linguists) who see web corpus construction as an act of sampling corpus documents from a population of web documents. In this case, it is vital to ask about the nature of the sampling process (for example its randomness), because it decides to a great deal how well insights gained from the sample generalize to the population. For example, as Schäfer and Bildhauer [2012] notice, in both the WaCky corpora and the COW corpora, a huge percentage of the crawled documents come from the web hosts which were already represented in the seed URLs, which were collected from search engine results (84% for deWaC, 56% for DECOW2012, and 95% for SECOW2011). This is suspicious, although not yet a proof that there is necessarily something wrong with the sampling procedure.

A further and maybe more serious illustrative example can be found by a simple query in the deWaC corpus. In this corpus, the second most frequent sequence of two tokens identified as proper names is *Falun Gong* with 51,641 occurrences. At the same time, the sequence *Gerhard Schröder* is ranked third with 24,481 (not even half as many) occurrences.[22] Since the corpus was probably crawled in 2005 (maybe 2006) according to Baroni et al. [2009], the documents were collected during a time when Gerhard Schröder was still chancellor of Germany or had just resigned. Table 2.10 compares the deWaC counts of the two sequences with the 2005 and 2006 stratum of the DeReKo newspaper reference corpus by the *Institut für Deutsche Sprache* [Kupietz et al., 2010], which is widely used by corpus linguists working on German.

This shows that the frequencies of certain proper names (and therefore most likely the distribution of topics) in the deWaC do not generalize to their frequencies in any kind of relevant population. The crawling procedure is clearly the most likely cause of such strange results. Researchers for whom such questions are irrelevant (maybe some computational linguists) can skip this section entirely. However, the selection of sampling procedures is also relevant in web characterization and related fields, cf. for example Becchetti et al. [2006]. For all other readers, this

---

[22]deWaC was processed with the TreeTagger (cf. Section 4.7). Since the tagger did not recognize all occurrences of *Falun Gong* as proper names, we give the corrected figures here, i. e., the number of all occurrences, whether they were recognized as proper names or not.

Sequence	deWaC		DeReKo 2005		DeReKo 2006	
Gerhard Schröder	15.05	(24,481)	61.77	(6,325)	10.04	(1,329)
Falun Gong	31.74	(51,641)	0.15	(15)	0.12	(16)

Figure 2.10: Comparison of the counts per million tokens (total count in parentheses) in deWaC (1.62 billion tokens) and the DeReKo strata for 2005 (132 million tokens) and 2006 (164 million tokens) for *Falun Gong* and *Gerhard Schröder*. The DeReKo archive used was *W-öffentlich*, release *DeReKo-2012-II*.

section sheds some light on the possible influence of the selection of the crawling strategy on the composition of the corpus.[23] By the crawling strategy, we mean the algorithm by which we penetrate the web graph, i. e., how we select links to queue and harvest, and in which order we follow them. A fundamental distinction [Gjoka et al., 2011] is between graph traversal techniques (each node is only visited once) and Random Walks (nodes might be revisited). We coarsely refer to all these strategies as crawling.

The simplest and most widely used crawling strategy (tacitly assumed in the previous sections) is breadth-first, a traversal technique. In a pure breadth-first crawl, all links are harvested and queued in the order they are found, using the URL Seen Test to avoid multiple queueing. Parallelization and politeness restrictions often cause local deviation from pure breadth-first. But despite these limitations, Mohr et al. [2004], for example, call the default queuing strategy in Heritrix breadth-first. The questions we need to ask are:

1. Does breadth-first introduce problematic sampling biases?
2. Is breadth-first a good maximizer of the *WC*?
3. Are there alternative strategies, and are they efficient enough to be used for the construction of large corpora?

It should be noticed that these questions will lead to superficially contradictory answers. For example, breadth-first might introduce sampling biases, but it might at the same time be the only option for the construction of very large corpora. In general, there is no single perfect strategy independent of the design goals of the corpus. We discuss these questions in Sections 2.4.2 and 2.4.3.

2.4.2   BIASES AND THE PAGERANK

If a sampling process is conducted in a way that does not produce the intended distribution, it is biased. For sampling from the population of web documents (cf. Section 2.2), the most neutral definition of an unbiased sample would be a sample according to a discrete uniform random distribution, i. e., one where each page has an equal chance of being sampled. Even if this is not

---

[23]Obviously, another factor is the selection of seed URLs, which was covered in Section 2.3.5.

the goal for all web corpus designers (cf. also Section 2.4.3), in this section, we first explain that more or less naïve crawling leads to potentially undesirable biases and definitely does not give each page an equal chance of being sampled. This poses a problem because our sample is usually such a small portion of the whole web that, if it is not a uniform random sample, we cannot be sure to have obtained a representative sample in any sense. Put differently, if we have taken only a very small non-uniform sample, we do not know whether the relevant documents are included. This is entirely independent of our definition of what a relevant document is. Even if we are ultimately not interested in a uniform random sample from the documents on the web (but, for example, a sample biased toward longer documents containing coherent text), the sampling method should not introduce other arbitrary and uncontrollable biases.

Many papers study the effectiveness of crawling strategies as the task of finding pages with a high PageRank early and of finding a large enough segment of the important pages from the whole web at all.[24] Such papers include Abiteboul et al. [2003]; Baeza-Yates et al. [2005]; Cho and Schonfeld [2007]; Fetterly et al. [2009]; Najork and Wiener [2001]. It was found that breadth-first manages to find relevant pages (pages with a high in-degree) early in a crawl [Najork and Wiener, 2001]. In Abiteboul et al. [2003], Online Page Importance Computation (OPIC) is suggested, basically a method of guessing the relevance of the pages while the crawl is going on and prioritizing URLs accordingly. In Baeza-Yates et al. [2005], several strategies are compared specifically for large intranet or TLD crawls, and breadth-first is evaluated as inferior to OPIC and other strategies.[25]

Now, since our goal is not search engine design but web corpus construction, we might want to look for sampling methods that allow us to correct for biases toward pages with a high in-degree or PageRank. In order to correct for a bias, its mathematical properties must be known. In a series of theoretical and experimental papers [Achlioptas et al., 2005; Kurant et al., 2010, 2011; Maiya and Berger-Wolf, 2011], it was found that breadth-first is biased toward pages with high in-degrees, but that this bias has not (yet) been mathematically specified. In non-exhaustive breadth-first samples from a graph, the distribution of in-degrees is distributed by a power law, even if the distribution in the graph from which the sample was taken is entirely different, for example a Poisson distribution [Achlioptas et al., 2005]. This is bad news, because it means that if we rely on breadth-first crawling for web corpus construction, we do not know exactly what we are doing and what population of documents the corpus represents. All we know for sure is that in the crawled set of documents (ultimately, the corpus), the in-degrees of the documents follow a power law.

So far, the linguistically oriented web corpus construction community does not seem to have paid much attention to this, but breadth-first sampling does have potentially problematic properties. As an example, Kornai and Hálacsy [2008] spend a few pages comparing the data rate at which different crawlers operate on their machines, and describe their own crawler as follows:

---

[24]The PageRank is a metric based on the in-degree designed to measure the in-degree in a more balanced way, and it will be introduced further below in this section.
[25]The Nutch crawler comes with an OPIC implementation.

We do not manage at all, let alone concurrently, link data, recency of crawl per host, or URL ordering. This simplifies the code enormously, and eliminates nearly all the performance problems that plague heritrix, nutch, larbin and other highly developed crawlers where clever management of such data is the central effort. [Kornai and Hálacsy, 2008, 9]

A year earlier, Issac [2007] presented a crawler for web corpus construction, which is clearly described as a naïve breadth-first system, without even mentioning the term breadth-first.[26] Given the aforementioned problems with small breadth-first sampling from largely unknown populations, such approaches seem quite cavalier. However, some corpus designers explicitly state that they are not interested in unbiased sampling, e. g.:

> [...] obtaining a sample of unbiased documents is not the same as obtaining an unbiased sample of documents. Thus, we will not motivate our method in terms of whether it favors unbiased samples from the web, but in terms of whether the documents that are sampled appear to be balanced with respect to a set of deliberately biased samples. [Ciaramita and Baroni, 2006, 127f]

In this tradition, the goal of web corpus construction is to obtain a corpus which shows a degree of variation (e. g., in terms of genres) comparable to the BNC, for example. However, Ciaramita and Baroni [2006, 131] mention unbiased sampling as possible future work.

Luckily, for a number of crawling strategies, the bias of the sampling method is known, and there are counter-measures to take. If we know that a crawling technique brings about a bias toward pages with a high Page/Rank, then we can try to compensate for the bias, i. e., calculate a metric and use it to adjust the probability of being sampled for each page. This is the case with specific types of Random Walks, which are known to be biased toward pages with a high PageRank. Already in Henzinger et al. [2000], a method for performing Random Walks through the web and correcting for the PageRank bias using a simple form of rejection sampling was suggested. Later papers describe other strategies and characterize them mathematically, often testing it on networks which are similar but not identical to the web, like online social networks (OSN) or peer-to-peer networks (P2P), e. g., Gjoka et al. [2011]; Rusmevichientong et al. [2001]. A major difference between the web and, for example, many OSN graphs is that the web is directed (i. e., there is no way of determining $I(p)$ for a page p), while OSNs are often undirected. This means that some of the strategies explored in such papers cannot be applied to web crawling without significant overhead.

We now describe the reasonably simple approach by Henzinger et al., which is based on a crawling strategy that has a known PageRank bias, which is then corrected for. The main problem with PageRank bias correction is that it is impossible to calculate the PageRank online at crawler runtime, and that offline PageRank calculations require significant resources. For efficiency reasons, the PageRank can therefore be estimated, be it offline or online. First, we need to briefly

---

[26]What is more, both crawlers are likely to violate politeness conventions and ignore Robots Exclusion. Kornai and Hálacsy actually mention that they were—at least at the time—not using *robots.txt* information.

explain the PageRank itself. It was introduced in Brin and Page [1998] and is one of the key ideas behind the success of Google's search engine. The key ideas of the PageRank are:

1. The PageRank of a page is high if it is linked to by many pages with a high PageRank.
2. Pages with few outlinks contribute more to the PageRanks of the pages they link to.
3. The PageRank $PR(p)$ of a page p is the equilibrium probability that a Markovian random walker through the web graph is on page p.

Point 3 is based on the idea that the PageRank models the behavior of a human web surfer who starts with an arbitrary page. The surfer would then click on a randomly selected out link on the current page repeatedly, effectively performing a Random Walk through the web graph. There remains, however, a certain probability that the surfer loses interest in the current route and, instead of clicking on a random link, starts all over with a new arbitrary page (like a bookmark or a search engine query result). The long-standing assumption in the search engine sphere is that PageRank or variants of it are useful in maximizing the WC of a crawl (pages with high PageRank should be crawled early), because these are the pages a search engine user would find most relevant to a query matched by these pages.

Mathematically, from each page p, the walker follows a random member of the set $O(p)$ of pages linked to by p with a fixed probability $(1-d) \div |O(p)|$, or jumps to a random page with probability d. Values for d are usually assumed to be between 0.10 and 0.15. The PageRank $PR(p)$ of a page p is defined as follows, where $I(p)$ is the set of pages linking to p and N the number of pages in the whole graph:

$$PR(p) = \frac{d}{N} + (1-d) \sum_{q \in I(p)} \frac{PR(q)}{|O(q)|} \tag{2.4}$$

Actual calculations of PageRank involve intermediate-level linear algebra and are beyond the scope of this introduction, but there is a short introduction in Manning et al. [2009] and an accessible introduction in Bryan and Leise [2006]. There are numerous software packages available to calculate the PageRank for a simulated or empirically observed graph, such as `igraph` (which includes Python and R interfaces).[27]

A PageRank-based Random Walk crawler needs to have a start URL and keep a certain amount of jump URLs (roughly equivalent to the seed URLs) to which it can jump with probability d (or when it reaches a page in OUT). Otherwise, it follows a randomly selected link from each page to another page, where the probability is $(1-d) \div |O(p)|$ for each link on p. For a toy graph, Figures 2.11 and 2.12 illustrate how a random jump changes the transition probabilities for a Random Walk through the graph.

Turning back to bias correction according to Henzinger et al. [2000], they estimate the PageRank $PR(p)$ via the visit ratio $VR(p)$, where L is the length of the crawl (number of transitions made) and $V(p)$ the number of visits to p during the crawl:

[27]http://igraph.sourceforge.net/

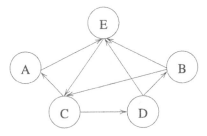

Figure 2.11: A simple web-like directed graph.

	A	B	C	D	E
A	0	0	0	0	1
B	0	0	0.5	0	0.5
C	0.5	0	0	0.5	0
D	0	0.5	0	0	0.5
E	0	0	1	0	0

	A	B	C	D	E
A	0.03	0.03	0.03	0.03	0.88
B	0.03	0.03	0.455	0.03	0.455
C	0.455	0.03	0.03	0.455	0.03
D	0.03	0.455	0.03	0.03	0.455
E	0.03	0.03	0.88	0.03	0.03

Figure 2.12: Transition probabilities for Figure 2.11 without and with random jumps (transition from row to column), $d = 0.15$.

$$PR(p) \approx VR(p) = \frac{V(p)}{L} \qquad (2.5)$$

This means that in practice, we have to allow for revisits, lowering the efficiency of the crawl. After the crawl is finished, the final sample is taken from the crawl, where the probability of the page being sampled from the crawl is inversely proportional to its VR, i. e., its estimated PR. After the procedure, the probability that a page is sampled should be the same for all pages:

$$Pr(p \text{ is sampled}) = Pr(p \text{ is crawled}) \cdot Pr(p \text{ is sampled}|p \text{ is crawled}) \qquad (2.6)$$

They estimate the following for the first term of the right-hand side:

$$Pr(p \text{ is crawled}) \approx L \cdot PR(p) \approx L \cdot VR(p) \qquad (2.7)$$

They state the following for the second term on the right-hand side:

$$Pr(p \text{ is sampled}|p \text{ is crawled}) \propto PR(p)^{-1} \qquad (2.8)$$

This just means that they sample from the results of the Random Walk using a skewed probability distribution over all crawled p such that the probability of drawing p is inverse to its (estimated) PageRank. Obviously, the final output in terms of the number of documents is lowered further by this post-crawl sampling procedure. Figure 2.13 shows a simple calculation for the pages $p_{1..6}$ encountered in a fictional crawl with $L = 10$.

Page	Visits	VR	VR^{-1}	Pr (sampled from crawl)
p_1	4	0.4	2.5	0.053
p_2	2	0.2	5	0.106
$p_3..p_6$	1	0.1	10	0.213

Figure 2.13: Sample calculation of PageRank bias correction for a toy PageRank Random Walk with $L = 10$.

As the authors themselves notice, a certain PageRank bias remains, most likely due to the inaccuracy of the PageRank estimation. The method has, however, the advantage of being relatively simple to calculate. In Rusmevichientong et al. [2001], a related method which the authors call Directed Sample is reported, which delivers unbiased samples, and which also does not require that the web be directed.

One disclaimer is in order: Any such advanced sampling is most likely not suitable if corpus size is of the essence, since Random Walks lead to a high number of page revisits (self-loops) and we cannot keep all pages we visited (e. g., if we sample all nodes from the simple Random Walk in Figure 2.13, then nothing would be gained). The Directed Sample algorithm by Rusmevichientong et al. [2001] introduces a significant crawling overhead to better estimate the in-degree of each page. For another method (Regular Sample), the authors report that in a sample of 2, 980, 668 nodes, 14, 064 were unique. If large corpora are required, some form of (maybe focused, cf. Section 2.4.3) breadth-first like technique is still the best option to choose.

To the best of our knowledge, the questions of how more advanced sampling methods affect the final web corpus, and how the size of the final corpus given a certain crawling effort can and should be balanced against the degree of validity of the sampling procedure, have not been examined for linguistically oriented web corpus construction. The next section introduces methods of steering the crawl toward desirable content, which is superficially the opposite of biasing.

2.4.3   FOCUSED CRAWLING

Finally, we mention ways of "biasing" a crawl toward desired pages, an advanced method to improve the WC for a well-defined weight function. Technically, this should not be called biasing (because it is a desired effect), although biasing and focusing bear certain similarities. The motivation for focusing a crawl in the context of web corpus construction is that we are usually looking for documents (i) in a certain language, (ii) which are not spam, (iii) do not contain predominantly binary media files (like audio or video portals), etc. This problem is totally distinct from the problem of graph-theoretical biases. A purely uniform random sample from the web contains a lot of material which we would not use in a corpus, just as much as a biased breadth-first crawl does. The idea of focusing is that we better make the selection as early as possible, i. e., ideally before a web page is requested. Originally, crawlers optimized to find documents according to genres, languages, etc., are called scoped crawlers, and focused/topical crawlers are a sub-type of scoped crawler looking for documents about certain subjects [Olston and Najork, 2010, 35]. We use the term "focusing" in a broader sense.

Focusing almost becomes a necessity when we build a corpus of a language that is not associated with a TLD (and which is not English). This is because, even if we use seed URLs pointing to pages exclusively in a certain language, a crawler following links by any unfocused strategy will very soon crawl documents in all sorts of languages (predominantly English). We have seen in Section 2.3.5 a strong influence of the seeds on the results in the very initial phase of the crawl, before it quickly moves too far away from the neighborhood of the seed URLs (esp. Figure 2.9). Relying on seed URL quality is thus not enough for specific crawling tasks, and we need a way of sustaining a high *WC* throughout the crawl.

Focused crawlers go back to Chakrabarti et al. [1999]. Usually, the links themselves within a document and the text in a window around the links are analyzed to come up with a prediction about the usefulness of the link given the crawl's scope or focus. Often, the relevance of the linking page itself or a larger link context are also included in the calculation. Various heuristics and machine learning methods are used for the calculation. An adequate coverage of the field is impossible to give here, but a selection of papers on the subject is: Almpanidis et al. [2007]; Chakrabarti et al. [1998]; Cho et al. [1998]; Gomes and Silva [2005]; Menczer et al. [2004]; Safran et al. [2012]; Srinivasan et al. [2005]. For language detection based only on URLs, probably the most important kind of detection required for web corpus construction, see Baykan et al. [2008]. For topic and genre detection from URLs, see Abramson and Aha [2009]; Baykan et al. [2009].

A simple method which cannot be called focusing in a strict technical sense is described in Suchomel and Pomikálek [2012].[28] The authors integrate their post-processing (roughly the steps described in Chapter 3) into their own crawler and collect statistics about the final yield from each encountered host (like the out/in ratio from Section 2.3.5, esp. Figure 2.9, but calculated per host). Hosts receive a penalty for low yield, up to a point where they get effectively blacklisted. From the information in the paper, it appears that the crawler implements a breadth-first strategy otherwise. Although the effect in *WC* maximization is moderate (as reported by the authors), the method is suitable for collecting more corpus data in a shorter time. Since it is a breadth-first system with online host blacklisting, the biases of this sampling method are quite difficult to characterize, however. It is not focused crawling in that it does not actively favor the discovery of relevant pages/hosts, but merely blacklists irrelevant pages/hosts.

---

[28]The crawler is available as SpiderLing: http://nlp.fi.muni.cz/trac/spiderling/

SUMMARY

Data collection is the simplest step in web corpus construction, in the sense that it can be decomposed into the two simple steps: (i) get some seed URLs and (ii) run the crawler. However, the pages which are crawled are a sample from a population (the web documents), and the sampling procedure pre-determines to a large extent the nature of the final corpus. We have introduced the steps which have to be taken, like seed URL collection and crawler configuration, but we have also given hints about the major decisions which corpus designers make when they select a crawling strategy, even when selecting a specific piece of crawler software. To this end, we have discussed the structure of the web itself as well as crawling strategies. Some strategies lead to larger corpora—like breadth-first crawling, maybe even with focusing. Some will deliver significantly smaller corpora for the same effort—like Random Walks with sampling bias correction—but will be free of sampling biases. In any case, we have only covered the collection of raw data so far, which needs to undergo diverse post-processing steps as described in Chapters 3 and 4.

CHAPTER 3

Post-Processing

3.1 INTRODUCTION

By post-processing, we refer to the non-linguistic cleanups which are required to turn the collection of downloaded HTML documents into a collection of documents ready to be included in a corpus. This involves cleanups within the documents and the removal of documents which do not meet certain criteria. The end product of the post-processing chain is often simply a set of plain text documents. Of course, putting all raw HTML files without the post-processing as described in this chapter into the corpus is hypothetically also an option. In this case, the corpus query engine should be capable of rendering HTML in order to make the corpus readable for humans, which is of course an achievable task. The real problem with keeping the HTML documents is, however, not the bad human-readability of HTML code, but the problems of linguistic post-processing and the statistics which will be derived from the corpus:

1. Tokenizers (Section 4.2) and all subsequent tools which add linguistic annotation expect text only, no HTML markup, scripts, etc. If we do not strip the HTML code (Section 3.2.1), we have to make sure these tools only see the natural language text from the web document.

2. The documents are encoded in different character encodings (both Unicode and non-Unicode), which is difficult to index, search, and display if we do not convert all documents to one encoding (Section 3.2.3).

3. A lot of text on web pages is redundant, non-content text, for example navigational elements, copyright notices, ads. If we do not remove this so-called boilerplate material (Section 3.3), statistics like word counts, sentence lengths, etc., will be distorted. See Chapter 5 about the problems which arise even because of the error rate of automatic boilerplate removal.

4. Not all pages are (predominantly) in the desired language. It is a good idea to remove documents which have no or only a small portion of text in the target language (Section 3.4). This includes documents which contain words in the target language, but not sentences. Such cases include tag clouds, lists of references or lists of names (e. g., signers of a petition).

5. Finally, many of the documents which the crawler downloads are duplicates of other documents, or they are very similar to other documents. Again, if we do not detect and remove them (Section 3.5), statistics derived from the corpus might be completely off.

In this chapter, we describe ways of implementing such cleanups. It should be kept in mind that each step involves design decisions, much like the selection of a crawling strategy (Chapter 2) does. The nature of the final corpus changes according to what is removed from and what is left in the corpus.

Having read through this chapter, readers should:

1. know about the structure and encodings used in (X)HTML and XML documents, and how to remove the markup using their own implementation or available tools and libraries,
2. have a good idea about what defines boilerplate on a web page, and how it is possible to detect and remove it,
3. know about the sources of perfect and near duplication and inclusion in web pages, and how duplication can be removed from a corpus (one method is described in enough detail for self-implementation).

3.2   BASIC CLEANUPS

3.2.1   HTML STRIPPING

In this section, we discuss the most basic and necessary cleanup step, namely markup removal. We speak of HTML removal consistently, but XML removal is a virtually identical task. In fact, there is a version of HTML (XHTML) which is based on XML. Formal specifications of HTML can be found in the archives of the World Wide Web Consortium or W3C (the organization which is responsible for all web-related standardizations), where primarily HTML 4.0, HTML 4.01, and HTML 5 are of interest, secondarily also XHTML and XML.[1]

An HTML document is a text document which consists entirely of HTML elements, which for the purpose of HTML removal can be classified as follows:

1. elements with enclosing tags and literal text in between of the form:
   `<tag> literal text </tag>`,
2. empty elements of the form:
   `<tag>` (not in XHTML) or `<tag></tag>` or `<tag />` (XHTML abbreviation),
3. elements which contain special, non-literal data, mostly `<script></script>` tags for script to be executed in the browser,

Elements can have attributes (which usually have values) which are added to the opening tag in the form `<tag attribute="value">`, where the value is always included in single or double quotes. Elements can be nested.

To remove well-formed HTML without preserving any of the document structure, it suffices to remove all tags in `<...>` and also remove the text in `<script></script>` and similar elements. Almost no parsing in the proper sense is required for this. A tentative list of elements which can be removed entirely is:

- `<script></script>` (usually JavaScript)

[1]http://www.w3.org/

- `<style></style>` (inline CSS)
- `<head></head>` (header, contains a lot of other invisible elements)
- `<form></form>` (form data is rarely desirable corpus content)
- `<applet></applet>`, `<object></object>`, `<embed></embed>` (binary content)
- `<code></code>` (programming code or similar)
- `<pre></pre>` (pre-formatted literal text, often—but not always—code examples)

HTML 5 brings a range of new elements which can be removed entirely, such as:

- `<audio></audio>` and `<video></video>` (media inclusion)
- `<track></track>` (multimedia annotation)
- `<figure></figure>` (floating figures)

HTML 5 also introduces more difficult-to-handle elements, like the `<ruby></ruby>` element. It is used to layout pronunciation information for East Asian characters, material which creators of Japanese corpora, for example, might not want to discard, but for which the alignment with the original characters must be preserved without interrupting the sequence of these original characters. Naïve HTML stripping is complicated by such features, and probably the best way of dealing with it is the implementation of separate HTML 4 and HTML 5 strippers.

A more principled way of removing HTML is by using a DOM (Document Object Model) parse of the document. The DOM is a standardized API specification for representing full parses of (X)HTML and XML documents and for dynamic updates of the contents of the parse by scripts.[2] It was designed as a standard to be implemented by rendering clients (primarily web browsers), but most modern programming languages offer a DOM library which can be used to get a parse of markup documents. DOM implementations which conform to the standard should be identical in their behavior (except for notational variants of the underlying programming language).

The document is parsed into a tree structure composed of objects (data structures) representing tree nodes, which are aware of their local context in the tree (mother and daughter nodes). For our purposes, a DOM parse can be regarded as a tree with a `document` node as its root, which has several `element` daughter nodes, which have as daughters other `element` nodes, `attribute` nodes and `text` nodes, corresponding to the kind of markup contained in HTML documents as described above. For a markup fragment like the following, Figure 3.1 shows a DOM tree structure.

```
<document>
  <element1 attribute1 attribute2>
    text
  <element1>
  <element2 ...>
```

[2]`http://www.w3.org/DOM/`

```
        . . .
    </element2>
    . . .
</document>
```

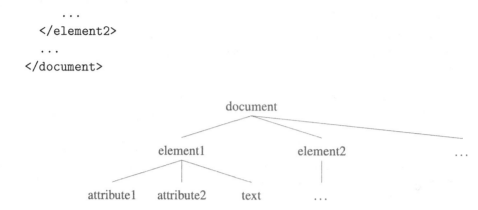

Figure 3.1: Structure of the DOM parse of a document.

To remove markup, it is feasible to obtain a full DOM parse from some library, then traverse the tree and extract all `text` nodes. Whether the overhead of the DOM parse and the tree traversal (compared to flat stripping) is acceptable, depends on the speed requirements and the efficiency of the DOM parser which is used. It should be kept in mind that the robustness of any flat or structured method of parsing HTML depends on the correctness of the markup. Unfortunately, HTML as found on the web often does not conform to the expected standards. This is mostly because web browsers are quite fault-tolerant when rendering HTML, such that errors in the markup are not visible to designers and visitors of the web page. Typical errors include non-closing tags, spaces between < and the tag identifier (`< tag>`), attribute values which are not in quotes (admissible but not recommended in plain HTML), overlapping tags (`<tag1><tag2></tag1></tag2>`), all sorts of attribute quoting errors (e. g., `<tag attribute="value>`), etc.

Both in flat and DOM approaches to markup removal, such error conditions can have serious consequences. In the worst case, markup can end up in the final corpus, which might be considered worse than non-markup text which is lost. One way to deal with such erroneous input is to use an HTML validator as offered by the W3C and discard faulty documents.[3] Since this reduces the number of documents in the corpus, another option is to use a program/library like `HTML Tidy` to fix incorrect HTML, as mentioned by Spousta et al. [2008].[4] Of course, if a DOM library is used, it might include some error correction, which should be checked before resorting to additional libraries like `HTML Tidy`. The time overhead of the extra cleanup step might be rewarded by higher accuracy in the subsequent steps, however.

Finally, for very simple approaches, off-the-shelf HTML strippers can be used. Since stripping other formats (like PDF and word processor formats) is significantly more complicated, such

---

[3]http://validator.w3.org/
[4]http://www.w3.org/People/Raggett/tidy/

tools are also a valid option if not just HTML documents are included in the corpus. Open source tools are available with many distributions of GNU/Linux, such as html2text, odt2text (Open Document Text format), pdftotext (from xpdf), and there are numerous commercial products available. Especially with monolithic HTML strippers, it should be checked which versions of HTML they convert correctly to avoid incorrect results. A disadvantage of monolithic tools is that we cannot extract features from the markup, which are needed, for example, in boilerplate removal (Section 3.3).

3.2.2   CHARACTER REFERENCES AND ENTITIES

An additional part of the diverse HTML specifications are character references and entities, beginning with & and ending with ; They are used to encode characters which cannot be represented in the normal encoding of the document (cf. Section 3.2.3). For example, the ISO-8859-1 character set, which is widely used for major European languages like English, German, Swedish, etc., cannot represent the Euro currency sign €. In ISO-8859-1 documents, content creators can insert it by the textual entity € instead of switching to another encoding (e. g., Unicode) for the document. Also, they are used to render literal versions of the protected characters of the markup (for example, < as < and > as >). For textual entities like € or ε for ϵ, translation tables have to be used to convert them to appropriate Unicode characters.

Alternatively, characters can be encoded by using numeric references to their Unicode codepoint (cf. Section 3.2.3). There is a decimal notation, introduced by &#, and a hexadecimal notation, introduced by &#x. For the € sign, we get € in decimal and € in hexadecimal notation. These can be converted directly by converting the string number representation to the corresponding integer, interpreting this as a Unicode codepoint, and inserting the corresponding Unicode character. This procedure assumes that the document is encoded as Unicode. If it is not, most of these references can only be deleted, which means that information from the original document is lost.

In real life, entities and references also come in faulty variants, where blanks after the & (& euro;) or before the ; (&euro ;) are quite frequent. Writing a robust entity converter is still a quite simple programming exercise, at least under the assumption that the document's target encoding is a Unicode encoding and all entities can be represented in the output. The next section gives a very brief overview of character sets, and argues that Unicode encodings should be used under any circumstances.

3.2.3   CHARACTER SETS AND CONVERSION

Letters and other characters need to be encoded numerically for electronic processing, i. e., each letter to be rendered or printed is encoded by a specific number, the codepoint. The document is a sequence of such numeric encodings. In this section, we sketch the important types of encodings, and how to convert between them. For many languages, web documents come in more than one encoding. For example, significant amounts of German documents under the .de domain come in UTF-8, ISO-8859-1, and Windows-1252. As the target encoding for all corpus documents, a Unicode encoding like UTF-8 is strongly recommended. UTF-8 is most widely used and offers the best trade-off between universal coverage of Unicode codepoints and size requirements for most languages. For a more in-depth coverage of character sets and encodings, any practical introduction to Unicode will do, such as Korpela [2006]. We only cover the basics here.

The encoding to which almost all standardized encodings today go back is ASCII. It is a 7-bit encoding, thus capable of representing 128 characters, of which some are control characters like tab (9) or newline (10). In terms of alphabets, it is just comprehensive enough for English texts. The layout of these 128 codepoints is still the same in all subsequent encodings.

To represent alphabets with additional characters (like French ç, German ä, Swedish å, etc.) 8-bit/1-byte encodings were introduced, which use the additional upper 128 codepoints to encode the other characters. Examples of such 1-byte encodings include ISO-8859 (Western), KOI-8 (Cyrillic), Windows-1252 (Western). To encode the huge number of East Asian characters, more complex multi-byte encodings were invented. Japanese documents can be encoded in at least three traditional encodings: JIS, Shift-JIS, and EUC. The basic idea of these encodings is to use sequences of bytes to encode codepoints which do not fit into a single byte. Thus, numerous alternative encodings emerged over time (some even vendor-specific), such that converter software needs to be aware of a lot of different translations.

The ISO-8859 family has 15 variants variants (1–16, 12 is undefined), where the upper block of 128 codes varies. However, ISO-8859-1 has the widest coverage of European languages among all ISO-8859 variants and was taken as the basis for the Unicode standards Universal Character Set 2 and 4 (UCS-2, UCS-4), where the numbers 2 and 4 stand for the number of bytes required to encode a codepoint. The Unicode initiative is the attempt to provide a single standard by which codepoints can be mapped to characters. The Unicode character sets were created such that the first 128 codepoints correspond exactly to ASCII, and the first 256 codepoints correspond exactly to ISO-8859-1 (which includes ASCII). UCS-2 adds one more byte and thus reaches a capacity of 65,536 codepoints in total; UCS-4 is a 4-byte encoding, allowing for hypothetical 4,294,967,296 characters (less in the actual standardization), of which the first 65,536 are identical to those in UCS-2. Figure 3.2 illustrates the inclusion relations between ASCII, ISO-8859-1, UCS-2, and UCS-4. This means that an ASCII document is a valid ISO-8859-1 document, an ISO-8859-1 document is a valid UCS-2 document, and a UCS-2 document is a valid UCS-4 document (but of course not the other way round). Problems are caused by all the traditional encodings, which often need to be mapped in more complex ways to UCS codepoints.

Additional complexity is added because UCS is usually encoded in the Unicode Transformation Formats UTF-8 and UTF-16. To write plain (untransformed) UCS-2 (or UCS-4), for example, each codepoint requires two (or four) bytes, which is a waste for the most frequent codepoints in European languages (namely the ASCII codepoints). To make the encoding more compact, a UTF-8 encoded document is a series of single bytes, and variable-length sequences of 1 to 4 bytes encode a single UCS codepoint. There are five different types of bytes, which can

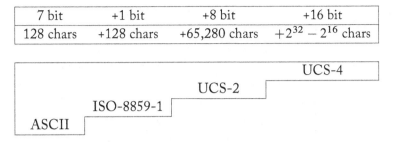

7 bit	+1 bit	+8 bit	+16 bit
128 chars	+128 chars	+65,280 chars	$+2^{32} - 2^{16}$ chars

Figure 3.2: Inclusion relations from ASCII to UCS-4.

be recognized by the bit sequence with which they begin. These five types are listed below, where each x can be 0 or 1. These x bits are used for the actual numerical encoding of the codepoint:

- a single byte: `0xxxxxxx`
- a byte that is first in 2-byte sequence: `110xxxxx`
- a byte that is first in 3-byte sequence: `1110xxxx`
- a byte that is first in 4-byte sequence: `11110xxx`
- a non-first byte in a sequence: `10xxxxxx`

Apart from the single byte starting with 0, all other types of UTF-8 bytes are part of a sequence with one of the sequence starting bytes and one to three following bytes. All bytes which do not conform to one of these types are invalid bytes in any UTF-8-encoded document.

Now, for example, the range from untranslated binary 10000000 (128–the 129th codepoint in 8-bit encodings) to 10111111 (191) cannot be represented by a single byte anymore, because the initial sequence 10 is reserved for following bytes in a sequence. From this it follows that UTF-8 is downward-compatible with ASCII, but not with ISO-8859 encodings, because ISO-8859 uses the range from 128 to 191 to encode characters. Instead, codepoint 128 has to be encoded in UTF-8 as 11000010–10000000 (194-128) and codepoint 191 as 11000010–10111111 (194-191), and similar for the rest of the codepoints up to 256. The maximum number of bits available for encoding codepoints is 21 in UTF-8, such that codepoints from 0 (as 00000000) to 2,097,151 (11110111–10111111–10111111–10111111) can theoretically be encoded. The types of admissible sequences are summarized in Figure 3.3.

first byte	full bitmask				byte length	bits available
`0xxxxxxx`				`0xxxxxxx`	1	7
`110xxxxx`			`110xxxxx`	`10xxxxxx`	2	11
`1110xxxx`		`1110xxxx`	`10xxxxxx`	`10xxxxxx`	3	16
`11110xxx`	`11110xxx`	`10xxxxxx`	`10xxxxxx`	`10xxxxxx`	4	21

Figure 3.3: UTF-8 sequences, where the x bits are used to encode the actual UCS codepoint.

No matter what the target encoding is, however, each downloaded document should be checked for its encoding and, if necessary, converted. There are two ways of detecting the encoding: either by relying on the encoding specified in the document header, or using a tool/library to detect it. Such software uses statistics of byte and byte sequence frequencies to guess the encoding of a document with a certain confidence. If the document declares its encoding, relying on the declaration is safer than using software to detect it. Usually, an HTML document should declare in its `<head></head>` element, a meta element such as this:[5]

```
<meta http-equiv="Content-Type" content="text/html;charset=iso-8859-1"></meta>
```

The HTML stripper (both flat and DOM based) can be easily modified to extract any such information from `<meta>` elements. The encoding might also have been transmitted in the `Content-Type` HTTP header, in which case the crawler must have written the headers to make the information accessible at post-processing time.

For character set detection, available libraries can be used. The most comprehensive and best supported is IBM's International Components for Unicode (ICU).[6] It has detection, conversion, regular expression matching for Unicode encodings, and even layout capabilities. Its detection function outputs the confidence at which a character set was detected, which is especially useful because the different ASCII-based 1-byte encodings are often difficult to tell apart. Of course, if an ISO-8859-15 document is recognized as ISO-8859-1, not too much harm will be done when it is converted to UTF-8, but incorrectly detected encodings are a source of noise. If the confidence is low, we might discard the document completely. Further free libraries and tools standardly available on `GNU/Linux` systems include the `iconv` tool and the `recode` library. Regular expression matching for UTF-8 is also offered by standard regular expression libraries like PCRE.

3.2.4   FURTHER NORMALIZATION

We now turn to some simple cleanups which could help to lower the level of noise and duplication in the corpus without too much effort. These are second-pass HTML and code removal, dehyphenation, reduction of repetitions, duplicate line removal, blanking of URLs, and other address information. There is probably more that could be done. It is always a good idea to look at the data (e. g., a random selection of a few thousand documents) and look for noise which can be fixed by such means.

Second-pass HTML (and script) removal might be necessary for the following reasons:

1. The HTML removal might have left traces of HTML in the corpus, usually as the result of faulty input documents.
2. There are a lot of pages on the web which are *about* HTML, scripting or programming languages, etc. Sometimes, code listings and examples are inserted into the literal text by

---

[5]For HTML 4, cf. http://www.w3.org/TR/html4/charset.html.
[6]http://site.icu-project.org/

means of entities, such that `<div>` is inserted as `&lt; div&gt;`, etc. Also, if `<pre></pre>` blocks have not been removed by default, these introduce a large number of code listings in the corpus.

The reason to remove such material is that it is not linguistically relevant material. If it is left in the corpus, tokens like *var* (C-style syntax) or *br* (HTML tag) will turn up as noise in the token lists, and some types might have increased token counts, such as *void* (C-style variable type, but also a word of English). We know of no off-the-shelf tool to perform such cleanups. We were successful with a simple strategy looking for JavaScript and CSS keywords as well as tag-like patterns and remove blocks/lines which contain such material in a high proportion. The threshold is, of course, a design decision and has to be determined heuristically for each corpus construction project.

Dehyphenation is the process of reconstructing pre-hyphenated words. For example, when people paste content from word processors into web content management systems, or when scanned documents processed with Optical Character Recognition (OCR) software are in the corpus, there might be hyphenated words at ends of lines. It is difficult to reliably infer ends of lines from HTML, so we should work under the assumption that information about them is not available. This means that naïve methods as described in Grefenstette and Tapanainen [1994] cannot work on the kind of data we encounter in web corpora.[7] The method basically consists in concatenating two strings if one occurs at the end of a line and ends in - and the next one occurs at the beginning of the following line. Actually, such simple approaches are dangerous even if ends of line are present, because such sequences can come from many sources, such as (with examples from our own UKCOW2011 corpus, a small test corpus of 890 million tokens):

1. true hyphenations (to be concatenated):

    • *It has a graph- ing facility for scatterplots*

2. words spelled with hyphens (also new creations) but with accidental space:

    • *any child whose self- esteem needs a boost*
    • *I called upon my Uranus- Neptune entity*

3. abbreviated coordinated compounds:

    • *mountain biking, horseriding, and hang- and paragliding*

4. dashes written as hyphens without spaces:

    • *some cases- and interpretation - of classic 1960s D-class movies*

There might be different or additional cases to consider depending on the language, and the frequencies of the different cases might vary in different languages. German has a very high occurrence rate of abbreviated coordinated compounds, for example.

---

[7]A data-driven method is superficially described in Zamorano et al. [2011], which is probably more promising.

Any dehyphenation software should be able to decide for any candidate string between one of the following edit actions:

1. **Merge**: Remove hyphen and concatenate both strings.
   graph- ing → graphing
2. **Concatenate**: Keep hyphen and concatenate both strings.
   self- esteem → self-esteem
3. **Dashify**: Insert a blank before the hyphen, optionally replace it with a dash.
   some cases- and interpretation → some cases—and interpretation
4. **Null**: Leave everything as it is.
   hang- and paragliding → hang- and paragliding

Using available dictionaries (maybe even hyphenation dictionaries) to perform a lookup in order to find out whether the candidate is a hyphenated word, is most likely not a promising approach in web corpus construction. Given the huge amount of noisy types in web corpora (cf. Chapters 4 and 5), and given the fact that in any natural language corpus, there is also a huge number of non-noisy types which are hapax legomena (words found only once), such approaches are not robust enough.

Possibly the best idea is to look at frequencies of unigrams and bigrams bootstrapped from the corpus itself and derive some kind of language model from it. In the case of *graph- ing*, for example, the frequencies of the following unigrams are of interest (with token frequencies (not case-sensitive) from UKCOW2011):

1. *graph-* $(f = 2)$
2. *graph* $(f = 10,026)$
3. *ing* $(f = 525)$
4. *graph-ing* $(f = 0)$
5. *graphing* $(f = 200)$
6. *graph- ing* $(f = 1)$

Notice that the token-frequencies of 1, 3, and 6 must always be greater or equal to 1 if *graph- ing* is in the corpus. Informally, any successful dehyphenation method should be able to detect that because of the low frequency of *graph-* and possibly also *graph- ing* compared to the relatively high frequency of *graphing*, the candidate should be merged. One problem is the high frequency of *ing*, which occurs in many hyphenated gerunds, such that *ing* as a token is actually far more frequent than the gerund *graphing*. To the best of our knowledge, no principled method has been described to work this out.

Reduction of repetitions concerns issues which will be dealt with again in Chapters 4 and 5. Especially in blogs, forums, etc., we find extremely long sequences of repeated characters. People make abundant use of certain punctuation characters like *??????????????, !!!!!!!!!!!* or mixed *!?!???!?!?!?!?!?!!!?*. Depending on how the tokenizer deals with such cases (cf. Section 4.2), they can be a considerable source of noise. For example, the tokenizer might split them into one token per character, which quite spoils the token count. Tokenizers probably react differently to repetitions of alphabetical characters such as in *ageeeeeeeeeeeeeeees* (from UKCOW2011), but under certain design goals, corpus designers might also want to remove or standardize such cases. Of course, some researchers might be interested specifically in such creative orthography, so removing or reducing such sequences is, again, a design decision. Reducing punctuation is quite simple. The `texrex` software suite, for example, has a mode in which any repetitions of punctuation characters are reduced to a sequence where each of the characters from the original sequence occurs only once, e. g., *!?!???!?!?!?!?!?!!!?* becomes *!?* For letter sequences, the graphemic rules of the target language can be used to reduce them to a reasonable length. Fortunately, spell-chekers like `GNU Aspell` are also good at fixing such cases (cf. Section 4.6), such that they might be used on these cases as part of the linguistic post-processing.

Potentially less of a difficult design decision is the **removal of duplicate lines or blocks**. Mainly (but not exclusively) in boilerplate parts of the web page, lines may appear multiple times in a row. They can be easily removed. However, it might be a good idea to do this after the deboilerplating algorithm has been applied, because it might change some of the metrics which are used for feature extraction in the deboilerplater.

The same is true for the last minor cleanup to be mentioned here: **blanking of URLs and email addresses**. Individual URLs and email addresses are usually not linguistically relevant and should be removed in order to protect privacy. More or less complete regular expressions can be construed, which find and replace such material. Since sometimes these addresses are used in sentences with an assignable part of speech, they should be replaced by some fixed string and not just removed. There are examples like (from UKCOW2011): *You may also e-mail him at editor@.overton-on-dee.co.uk.* It could be turned into something like: *You may also e-mail him at emailblank.* Replacing instead of removing such addresses allows the POS tagger (cf. Section 4.5) to guess a part-of-speech, which can under certain conditions improve the overall accuracy of the tagger.

A more difficult task is the removal of other address information, phone numbers, etc. Some of them (like phone numbers) can also be detected with reasonable accuracy by regular expressions. Street names and similar information are more difficult to recognize. However, addresses and email addresses often are located in boilerplate regions (together with copyright notices, etc.). Among the features extracted for boilerplate removal can be the number of email addresses, phone numbers, etc. Blanking out such information before the boilerplate remover does its job might reduce its accuracy. We now turn to boilerplate removal in Section 3.3.

3.3   BOILERPLATE REMOVAL

3.3.1   INTRODUCTION TO BOILERPLATE

We have described in Section 3.2.1 that HTML removal is essentially a trivial task. After a successful removal of the markup, only the text (without the graphics and other multimedia content) that would be visible in a version of the page as rendered in a web browser remains. This text, however, might contain parts that we do not want to include in a corpus. Figure 3.4 shows regions on a rendered page that are of such a nature.

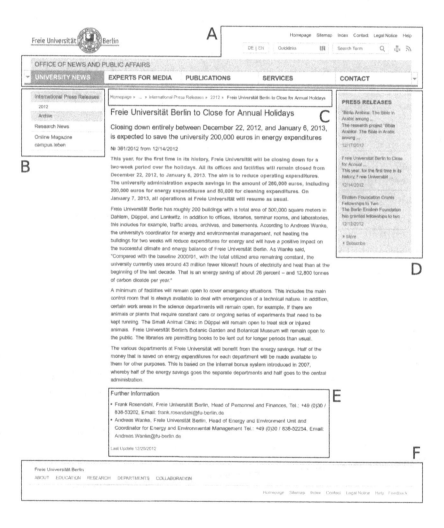

Figure 3.4: A web page with different regions of boilerplate marked.

The A region contains layers of navigational menus, which are auto-generated for each page of the institution. Especially with crawling strategies that tend to exhaustively download all documents served by a host, the bigramm *university news* could be overrepresented in the corpus. Even with better crawling strategies, typical menu words such as *homepage, sitemap, contact* could be overrepresented. Since it is content management systems which insert these words in such high numbers (and not humans producing them this often), removing menus is common practice in corpus construction.[8] Regions B and C are navigational elements which inform the user about her/his position within the navigation logic of the site. Region C contains what is usually called breadcrumb navigation. Region D holds linked content from the same content category (in this case, press releases). Such regions are especially problematic, because they often contain the beginning of the text of the linked document, broken off after a few words, usually in the middle of a sentence, maybe followed by *[Read more], (more),* …, etc. If not removed, such elements introduce redundant content (because these links occur many times on pages from the same server). Also, machine-truncated sentence fragments are linguistically of limited use. Region E consists of addresses (electronic and street addresses) and update information. As was mentioned in Section 3.2.4, such blocks can possibly be recognized by (among other things) the high number of email addresses which occur in them. Finally, block F contains a mirror of parts of the navigational menus.

The task of boilerplate removal is to automatically identify and remove the text in areas A–F, and leave only the actual text. The success of the respective method is measured using the customary metrics of Precision, Recall, and F.[9] Here, Precision is defined as the proportion of the correctly returned blocks, areas, sentences, etc. (whatever the chosen unit is) from the set of correctly and falsely returned such elements:

$$\text{Precision} = \frac{|\text{correctly returned}|}{|\text{correctly returned} \cup \text{falsely returned}|} \tag{3.1}$$

The Recall is defined as the proportion of the correctly returned blocks from the set of correctly returned and falsely deleted blocks (in other words the proportion of actually returned elements from the set of those elements which should have been returned):

$$\text{Recall} = \frac{|\text{correctly returned}|}{|\text{correctly returned} \cup \text{falsely deleted}|} \tag{3.2}$$

The *F* measure is the harmonic mean of the two and a measure to evaluate the overall quality of the algorithm:

$$F = 2 \cdot \frac{\text{Precision} \cdot \text{Recall}}{\text{Precision} + \text{Recall}} \tag{3.3}$$

[8]But notice that, of course, search engine providers are most likely not interested in indexing such content, either, and also perform boilerplate removal.
[9]Here and throughout, we use the term F as a shorthand for F_1.

We implicitly describe approaches to boilerplate removal for HTML 4 or older, as well as XHTML. HTML 5 introduces some features which might actually make boilerplate removal simpler and more reliable. It specifies elements such as `<header></header>` and `<footer></footer>` for document headers and footers, `<nav></nav>` for navigational areas, and even `<article></article>` for self-contained blocks which can be treated as single documents.

In the absence of such content- and structure-declaring markup, we have to find features of the markup and the text within a block which allow us to automatically classify it as either boilerplate or good text. We assume here that some kind of block boundaries were extracted in the HTML stripping process (cf. Section 3.2.1). With flat HTML stripping, splitting up the documents into blocks (which often correspond to natural language paragraphs) can be achieved by inserting block boundaries where certain tags occur. For example, we can insert block boundaries wherever `<p>`, `<br>`, `<div>`, and maybe some other tags (those which cause paragraph breaks in the rendered web page) occur. For those blocks, relevant features can be calculated (cf. Section 3.3.2), and those blocks which are found to be boilerplate based on those features can be removed. Alternatively, from a DOM tree, sub-trees which are classified as boilerplate can be removed. In this scenario, the document is stripped by traversing the tree and extracting text nodes, or by saving the stripped DOM tree as HTML again and sending it to some generic HTML stripper. Some contestants in the CLEANEVAL competition [Baroni et al., 2008] used such a method, finally sending the cleansed HTML document to the Lynx text-only browser, which can be used to strip HTML.[10] In DOM-based extraction, blocks correspond to sub-trees in the DOM tree (for example, all div and p elements).

There is no most natural or intrinsically best way of finding such blocks, and some approaches use fundamentally different techniques. For example, Gao and Abou-Assaleh [2007] use a computationally more expensive visually oriented DOM-based segmentation method, which tries to locate rectangular visible areas, roughly like the ones framed in Figure 3.4 (VIPS, Cai et al., 2003). Since many of the informative features for boilerplate removal come from the markup, using some markup-based block/area splitting is by far the most popular. We now describe the kind of features which are extracted for boilerplate detection in Section 3.3.2.[11]

3.3.2   FEATURE EXTRACTION

Automatic boilerplate removal (or deboilerplating) can be accomplished using heuristic weight calculation formulae [Baroni et al., 2009; Gao and Abou-Assaleh, 2007; Pomikálek, 2011]. More commonly, however, some form of (usually) supervised machine learning is used for this task. I. e.,

---

[10]http://lynx.isc.org/

[11]We do not discuss approaches which try to figure out templates used for whole sites, especially when content management systems (CMS) are used. Clearly, high accuracy in content extraction can be achieved if the template according to which a site's CMS formats its articles is known exactly. However, this approach is usually difficult and/or expensive to implement for huge web crawls not restricted to a limited number of hosts. Cf. Bar-Yossef and Rajagopalan [2002]; Chakrabarti et al. [2007] as entry points.

an algorithm has to be chosen which is capable of learning a binary decision (a block of text from the document is/is not boilerplate) from a set of training data annotated by humans, and the decision (as learned) should be generalizable from the training set to any new unknown data of the same type. The algorithm learns the decision based on a set of features which have to be extracted for each of the blocks in the training set and for the unknown data in a production run.

There have been a number of papers about boilerplate detection and removal. Most prominently, the CLEANEVAL competition [Baroni et al., 2008] produced a number of efforts, namely Bauer et al. [2007], Evert [2007], Gao and Abou-Assaleh [2007], Girardi [2007], Hoffmann and Weerkamp [2007], Issac [2007], Marek et al. [2007], Saralegi and Leturia [2007]. The WaCky corpora have undergone a very simple boilerplate removal method, which is nevertheless reported to be very effective [Baroni et al., 2009]. Based on Marek et al. [2007], Spousta et al. [2008] claim to have achieved a very high accuracy. Other approaches include Kohlschütter et al. [2010]; Pasternack and Roth [2009]. Recently, Pomikálek [2011] has developed yet another solution, including an online interface for quick evaluations.[12] Schäfer and Bildhauer [2012] also proposed a deboilerplater system as part of the `texrex` software package, which they report as being very fast while being also reasonably accurate.

We now present a selection of features, primarily ones used in the method by Spousta et al., because they use a very comprehensive feature set. Features are grouped into classes, and we will illustrate some of them immediately, using an analysis of the page depicted in Figure 3.4.[13]

- **Markup-related features**
    - tag class that started the block (e. g., `<div>`, `<p>`, etc.),
    - length of the markup in characters or bytes,
    - length of the non-markup text in characters or bytes,
    - ratio of markup and non-markup,
    - count of opening and closing tags,
    - count of anchor tags/links (`<a>`),

- **Stop words etc.**
    - count of email addresses and URLs in the literal text,
    - count of stop words or phrases,
    - number of copyright (©) or similar characters typical of boilerplate regions,

- **Graphemic features**
    - count/ratio of numbers in the text,
    - count/ratio of uppercase/lowercase letters in the text,
    - count/ratio of punctuation/non-punctuation characters in the text,

---

[12]`http://nlp.fi.muni.cz/projekty/justext/`

[13]It should be mentioned that there are also attempts at deboilerplating that work without any of the markup related features as mentioned here, but rely entirely on features of the natural language text, e. g., Evert [2007].

- **Linguistically motivated features**

  – block ends in a sentence-final punctuation character (at least [.?!]),
  – count of sentences,
  – average sentence length,
  – average word length,
  – confidence of a language identifier that the text is in the target language,

- **Whole-document features**

  – length of the whole document with/without markup,
  – overall ratio of markup/non-markup,

Obviously, all these features require little or no linguistic processing. Other features, which do require such processing, are conceivable. Each block could be run through a parser, for example, to see for how many sentences in the block the parser finds a parse. At least intuitively, if the parser finds a lot of sentences for which there is a parse, the chances of the block containing a list of menu items is quite low. The performance penalty would be severe, however: Since deduplication (Section 3.5) works better on documents which have already been cleansed from boilerplate, it is better to apply deboilerplating before deduplication. This means that the number of documents is still very high at this stage, and the documents often contain many more boilerplate blocks than text blocks. The amount of text which would have to be parsed is thus very high, which can quickly lead to days and weeks of extra processing time. This is true for all more expensive feature extraction and machine learning methods, even if they are not as expensive as parsing. For example, Spousta et al. [2008] achieves quite good results with over 40 features and Conditional Random Fields: *Precision* $= 0.81$, *Recall* $= 0.8$, $F = 0.8$. An efficiency of 300,000 documents per CPU day is reported, which might already be too slow in some situations. The cost of extra features or more expensive algorithms must therefore be balanced very carefully against the added accuracy, which can be measured using the standard metrics of Precision, Recall, and F.

Figures 3.5 and 3.6 exemplify and visualize the usefulness of certain features. The sentence count (a) goes up in the text region, so does the average sentence length (b). The proportion of the markup (c) approaches zero in the text region; clearly, there are a lot of anchor tags and more design-specific markup in the non-text regions, causing the proportion of markup to be higher. The percentile in the text body (d) is an interesting feature. It is percentile in/proportion of the whole non-markup text reached at the end of the block. As it is, it helps the deboilerplater to identify the beginning and the end regions of the document, where there is usually only boiler-plate. But clearly, the text mass grows only very slowly in the boilerplate regions, but rapidly in the text regions. This might be informative for approaches which seek to extract coherent larger areas of text, possibly accepting small amounts of boilerplate in the middle. Visually, the propor-tion of letters within the text (e) is not very informative in this example (which does not mean it is uninformative in general). The proportion of lowercase (vs. uppercase) letters (f) is consistently

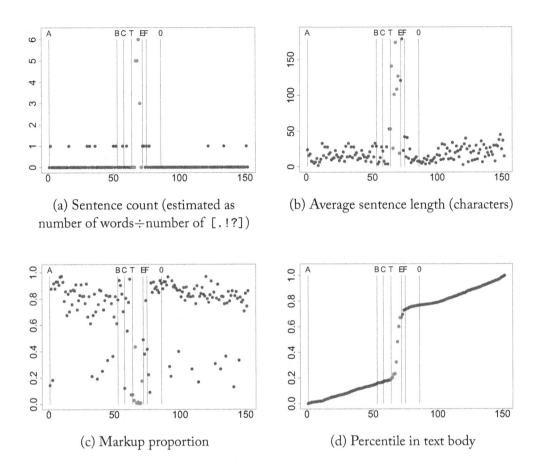

(a) Sentence count (estimated as
number of words÷number of [.!?])

(b) Average sentence length (characters)

(c) Markup proportion

(d) Percentile in text body

Figure 3.5: Distribution of some deboilerplater features extracted for the page in Figure 3.4, labels are at the top. The x-axis is the n-th block, block boundaries were inserted at certain tags like `<div>` and `<p>`. The vertical lines mark the beginnings of the regions from Figure 3.4; T marks the beginning of the text region; 0 is material hidden by scripts and thus invisible in the rendered version; region D is inserted by scripts and does not appear in the HTML source.

higher in the text region, and the proportion of punctuation characters (g) might be significantly raised. Finally, the number of anchor tags per character is consistently low.

Even in this illustrative example, there are certain jumps of some values between the blocks in the non-boilerplate region. There are also boilerplate blocks with at least some values being more indicative of non-boilerplate areas. As we mentioned, these and other or similar features are fed into some kind of machine learning software or used in heuristics for some non-machine

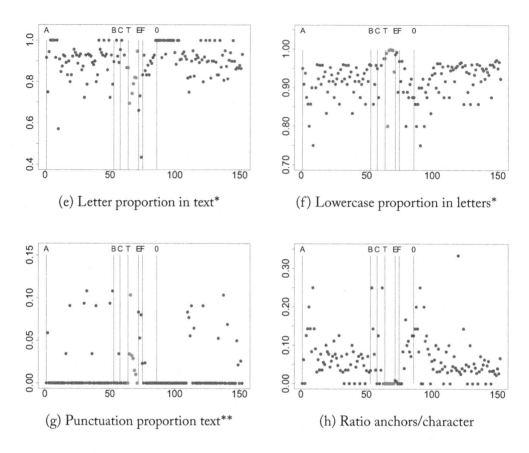

(e) Letter proportion in text*

(f) Lowercase proportion in letters*

(g) Punctuation proportion text**

(h) Ratio anchors/character

Figure 3.6: Continuation of Figure 3.5. * Some low-end outliers are invisible. ** Some high-end outliers are invisible.

learning calculation of the goodness of the text in the block. Such accidental jumps in the values might lead to erratic deletions of blocks in the middle of good regions as well as scattered blocks of boilerplate remaining in the corpus when the machine learning algorithm is applied. To alleviate this, a method can be chosen which does not consider the blocks in isolation, but also uses the context of each block for the decision. For all other methods, the neighboring values for HTML tag density and similar values can be added to a block's feature set as additional features to achieve something similar. This will in the best case lead to a smoother distribution of the delete and keep decisions. In Section 3.3.3, we briefly mention some machine learning options which have been used.

3.3.3   CHOICE OF THE MACHINE LEARNING METHOD

All sorts of methods have been used in boilerplate removal:

- Decision Trees, Language Models, Genetic Algorithms (evolving a regular expression) in Hoffmann and Weerkamp [2007],
- naïve (in the words of the author) Language Models in Evert [2007],
- Support Vector Machines (SVM) in Bauer et al. [2007],
- Conditional Random Fields (CRF) in Marek et al. [2007]; Spousta et al. [2008],
- Naïve Bayes Classifier in Pasternack and Roth [2009],
- Multi-Layer Perceptron (MLP) in Schäfer and Bildhauer [2012].

There is no general recommendation, because the choice of algorithm (or decision to use just some heuristics/hand-crafted formula) depends on the requirements for a given task, including such considerations as the number of documents which have to be processed in which span of time, the available machine power, the kind of web pages to be processed, maybe even the programming language used for the project. Some methods are more accurate than others, given the extracted features. Some algorithms require features with certain levels of measurement or scalings. Sometimes, performance is of the essence, and some accuracy can be traded in.

For software systems which are redistributed to other users, additional considerations might play a role. For example, since accuracy must be evaluated in terms of precision (roughly: the better the precision the cleaner the corpus) and recall (roughly: the better the recall the more complete are the documents), implementations which allow end-users of the software product to adjust precision and recall for pre-trained models offer an additional value. The Multi-Layer Perceptron used Schäfer and Bildhauer [2012] and the texrex software is of such a nature. The Perceptron itself calculates for each paragraph a value between 0 (low probability that it is boilplate) and 1 (high probability that it is boilerplate). To arrive at a binary classification, a threshold somewhere between 0 and 1 has to be applied. If a clean corpus is more important than complete documents, the threshold can be set to a higher value, and vice versa. Figure 3.7 plots the precision and the recall according to threshold settings between 0 and 1.

In any given project, it might be a good idea to benchmark various learning algorithms, feature sets, and training data sets to find the best configuration in terms of accuracy and efficiency. An excellent tool to test many machine learning approaches effectively and systematically is Weka [Hall et al., 2009], which is used also in the comprehensive introductory book by Hall and Witten [2011].[14] The RapidMiner tool also offers a huge number of algorithms, including data transformations.[15] Other available comprehensive machine learning applications and libraries have other advantages. For example, the Apache Mahout library is integrated with Apache Hadoop to allow for easy parallelization on clusters of machines.[16]

---

[14]http://www.cs.waikato.ac.nz/ml/weka/
[15]http://sourceforge.net/projects/rapidminer/
[16]http://mahout.apache.org/

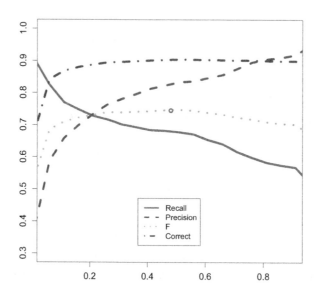

Figure 3.7: Precision, recall and F for the generic MLP from Schäfer and Bildhauer [2012], according to the cutoff/threshold above which blocks count as boilerplate. The x-axis is the threshold. $F_{max} = 0.75$ (marked with a dot) at Threshold = 0.48 with Precision = 0.83 and Recall = 0.68

Finally, one aspect of block-wise boilerplate removal should be considered. If the recall of the applied algorithm is lower than 1 (which it always is), then there are blocks missing which would have contained good corpus material. In the worst case (combined with block detection failure), a sentence spanning two blocks is truncated. This means that for certain types of linguistic research such as Information Structure (when givenness of discourse referents is important), the corpus might be unusable or at least of inferior quality. Also, in Information Extraction (e. g., distributional semantic approaches like LSA, Landauer et al., 1998) missing and broken contexts of words or sequences of words can lower the quality of the results. Corpus designers can consider the following options to deal with such problems:

1. Do not remove blocks arbitrarily, but keep blocks from a single window (possibly containing several blocks) for which the overall boilerplate level is minimized [Baroni et al., 2009].
2. Keep everything and annotate potential boilerplate as such.

Option 1 does not solve all aforementioned problems. From the linguistic side, it might matter that a discourse referent could still be introduced outside the selected window. This solution is also inadequate considering certain kinds of web document layouts such as forum layouts, which typically contain a constant alternation of boilerplate blocks (date and time of posting, user aliases, etc.) and normal text blocks (the actual forum posts), often in very long sequences. Option 2 massively increases the amount of data in the final corpus, but is in our view the only option for any kind of document-related linguistic research. It allows users of the final product to restrict queries and statistical analyses to the likely good blocks of the documents, but to see the boilerplate regions when required. This approach has not yet been implemented, as far as we know.

There are a number of readily available pieces of software which implement boilerplate removal, such as `boilerpipe`, `BootCaT`, `jusText`, `NCleaner`, `texrex`.[17,18,19,20,21]

This concludes the short introduction to boilerplate removal, and it leaves two major open tasks in the non-linguistic post-processing department. The first one is the task of identifying the language of the document, which is required both for monolingual corpora (filter out documents not in the target language) and multilingual corpora (assign a feature to each document which identifies its language). As it was said above, language identification could also be used as a feature in boilerplate removal (p. 52), and it could be used in focused crawlers (Section 2.4.3), but we now move on and describe the general method separately in Section 3.4.

3.4   LANGUAGE IDENTIFICATION

In this section, we will describe approaches to language identification very briefly. In the context of web corpus construction, language identification is required, because even if national TLDs are crawled or language guessing is already performed at crawl time based on URLs (cf. Section 2.4.3), there will always be documents in the crawl data which are not in the target language. Language identification is therefore yet another necessary cleansing procedure. The brevity of this section is mainly due to the fact that language identification has been around for quite a while and can be considered a stable discipline.

An early and very accessible paper summarizing the two main approaches is described in Grefenstette [1995]. The two approaches are based on (i) character n-gram statistics plus machine learning/language modelling or (ii) function word statistics. The majority of software developers as well as authors (compare early papers such as Cavnar and Trenkle, 1994; Dunning, 1994) favors the n-gram approach because it needs relatively little training data, is domain-independent (works on all kinds of texts from the target languages), and is quite accurate also on shorter strings.

Recently, identifying languages for very short texts like messages in microblogging systems or query strings has become a new focus of research. For example, cf. Carter et al. [2012]; Gottron and Lipka [2010]. However, some of the approaches to language identification in microblog posts use information external to the text (such as user profiles and linked user profiles), which

---

[17]http://code.google.com/p/boilerpipe/
[18]http://bootcat.sslmit.unibo.it/
[19]http://sourceforge.net/projects/webascorpus/files/NCleaner/
[20]http://code.google.com/p/justext/
[21]http://sourceforge.net/projects/texrex/

are not available in web corpus construction. Another problem very specific but not exclusive to web data is multilingual documents, i. e., documents which contain a mix of languages or, quite frequently, one dominant language with shorter blocks from another language (mostly English). A character n-gram approach is described in Teahan [2000], and in a more recent paper (which tries to resuscitate the word-based approach), Řehůřek and Kolkus [2009] also describe a method to achieve segmentation plus identification.

One task very much related to language identification, and which to our knowledge has received very little attention, is the detection of documents containing non-text. For example, many pages on the web contain tag clouds (isolated nouns, adjectives, and other lexical words), which end up as incoherent word lists in the corpus. Other examples are dictionary lists, lists of products or advantages of a product (maybe in the form of truncated noun phrases), or lists of signers of a petition. Such documents are often identified as being in the target language by standard tools based on character n-gram statistics, but many corpus designers would probably rather not have them in the corpus. The function word method is better suited to detect such documents, and for the WaCky corpora and the COW corpora, more or less heuristic methods were used to filter documents with few or no function words. The accuracy of both approaches has not been reported properly, so we leave out the details here. Since the common classification methods in language identification are supervised, however, they require a manually classified training input. This means that corpus designers need to operationalize what a non-text document is, which is not an easy task in our experience. To aggravate the situation, there are of course documents which contain "good" text along with tag clouds, lists, and foreign material in all kinds of proportions.

Finally, we would like to mention that there are many libraries and tools implementing the standard approaches to language identification available. Among the freely available ones which come packed with a lot of language models (more than 50) are `mguesser`, written in C, `language-detection`, written in Java, and `langid.py`, written in Python.[22],[23],[24]

3.5   DUPLICATE DETECTION

3.5.1   TYPES OF DUPLICATION

A huge number of the documents found on the web are not unique. Content creators copy from each other or buy content from the same sources (such as news agencies); some providers also serve the same content from different hosts, etc. Blogs and other content management systems create duplication very systematically by offering different views of the same content.

Systematically, we can say that duplication comes in the following types:

1. full duplication of documents (e. g., two servers generating content from one database),

---

[22]http://www.mnogosearch.org/guesser/
[23]http://code.google.com/p/language-detection/
[24]http://github.com/saffsd/langid.py/

Figure 3.8: Blog content management system introducing redundancy through multiple views of the same content. On the left is the homepage view containing the *n* most recent posts, including the post *Erotische Schriften*. On the right is the page with the individual view for the single post *Erotische Schriften*.[25]

2. partial duplication of documents (e. g., by quotation, plagiarism, etc.),
3. document inclusion (e. g., in blog systems as illustrated above in Figure 3.8),
4. in-document duplication (mostly forum threads with "Quote" function being used excessively).

We do not treat in-site duplication as a case of its own, because it is usually covered by one of the above types. In-site duplication occurs when bits of text occur on many pages of one site. If this happens, it is mostly caused by blog or CMS systems and a case of either partial duplication or inclusion. When detected in the final corpus, in-site duplication can also be indicative of insufficient boilerplate removal.

In Section 3.5.2, we describe the simple methods by which perfect duplicates can be detected, and in Section 3.5.3, we deal with the slightly more difficult matter of how to detect documents which share a lot of content and are quite similar. Both methods can be applied at any level. They can be applied to the sentences or blocks within a document, to documents of one host, or to a whole corpus of documents. The only thing that changes is the feasibility of a one-by-one comparison. While it is usually no problem (although inefficient) to compare the sentences from a document pairwise (because most documents are small enough), doing the same with all documents of a large corpus quickly becomes too time consuming.

As an example, assume the corpus is 10^7 documents large before deduplication. Pairwise comparison of documents means that we have to make

---

[25]From: http://www.lawblog.de/

$$\binom{10^7}{2} = 5 \times 10^{13} \tag{3.4}$$

comparisons. At a speed of $1\mu s$ per comparison, this will take almost 580 days. Thus, to do document comparison for large corpora, we need to break down the task such that it scales much better than pairwise comparison. Both types of duplicate detection can be performed in such a way.

However, what we do with the identified duplicates is, once more, a design decision. Within a document, duplicate paragraphs might be removed, maybe inserting a backreference to indicate to corpus users that there was a repeated paragraph (and which one it was). In document deduplication, we might decide to erase all except one randomly chosen document from each set of perfectly identical documents and to remove the shorter one of two near duplicates (to maximize the amount of text in the deduplicated corpus). In the original approach described in Section 3.5.3 [Broder et al., 1997], the goal of the authors was to cluster documents by similarity.

3.5.2 PERFECT DUPLICATES AND HASHING

Detecting perfect duplicates can be achieved by keeping hashes of documents already seen, and discarding documents with the same hash. A hash function calculates a numerical representation with a fixed bit length (a hash value) of another object (the key, in our case exclusively character strings/documents). Ideally, two different keys are rarely represented by the same hash value, and similar keys are not represented by similar hash values. If two non-identical keys accidentally have the same hash value, it is called a collision. As a general rule, the longer the hash value (in bits), the more rarely there is a collision.

Since for two identical documents any hash function calculates the same value, it suffices to keep a list of hashes of each document seen, simply discarding documents which have a hash value which is already known. The efficiency of the procedure depends on the total number of documents, the efficiency of the hash function, and the sorting/lookup algorithm used to store the hash values. The number of false positives (documents falsely discarded as documents) depends on the quality of the hash function and the hash length. Likely, using a Bloom Filter as described in Section 2.3.3 for the URL Seen Test will also provide the best compromise between accuracy and efficiency here.

However, even a single character missing, added, or changed in one of two otherwise identical documents, will lead to a false negative (two near duplicate documents being kept). This is because of the otherwise desirable property of hash functions that a similarity of the keys does not lead to similar or even identical hash values. To illustrate, assume the very short documents d_1 and d_2, only differing by a single comma:

$d_1 =$ *Yesterday we calculated a hash value efficiently and accurately.*
$d_2 =$ *Yesterday, we calculated a hash value efficiently and accurately.*

For example, the 32-bit Fowler–Noll–Vo hash function (FNV-1) produces the following entirely different hexadecimal values: $FNV1(d_1) = 5c517c3d$ and $FNV1(d_2) = e1235bef$.[26] Since a Bloom Filter is based on hashing, this problem will also affect Bloom Filter implementations. In Section 3.5.3, we introduce a standard method to detect such cases of near duplication.

3.5.3   NEAR DUPLICATES, JACCARD COEFFICIENTS, AND SHINGLING

To test whether two documents are quite similar, although not identical, we need a measure of document similarity. A straightforward such measure is the Jaccard Coefficient [Manning et al., 2009, 61]. It measures the similarity of two sets, such that we can derive the set of token n-grams from a document and compare the result. For example, the token bigram sets (call them bigram fingerprints F_2) of the documents d_1 and d_2 from Section 3.5.2 are as follows (non-identical members in bold print):

$$F_2(d_1) = \{\textbf{(Yesterday;we)}, (we;calculated), (calculated;a), (a;hash), (hash;value),$$
$$(value;efficiently), (efficiently;and), (and;accurately), (accurately;.)\}$$
$$F_2(d_1) = \{\textbf{(Yesterday;), (;we)}, (we;calculated), (calculated;a), (a;hash), (hash;value),$$
$$(value;efficiently), (efficiently;and), (and;accurately), (accurately;.)\}$$

The Jaccard Coefficient J of these sets is calculated as:

$$J(F_2(d_1), F_2(d_2)) = \frac{|F_2(d_1) \cap F_2(d_2)|}{|F_2(d_1) \cup F_2(d_2)|} = \frac{8}{11} \approx 0.73 \qquad (3.5)$$

We could now go on and determine a threshold for the Jaccard Coefficient, above which the shorter of the documents is erased from the collection. Of course, it is again impractical to calculate Jaccard Coefficients for all pairs of documents in a large collection (Section 3.5.1). The shingling approach suggested by Broder et al. [1997] therefore reduces the n-gram (n customarily between 4 and 6) fingerprint to a smaller but representative set of hash values, which can be sorted and processed in a linear fashion.[27] Here, we only describe the practical procedure for shingling without clustering. For the proofs and the extension to clustering, cf. Broder et al. [1997] and Section 19.6 from Manning et al. [2009]. For an overview and evaluation of other techniques, cf. Henzinger [2006].

The simplified shingling procedure without clustering can be decomposed into the following steps. We leave the question of how to hash the n-grams and how to select the representative hashes to be explained later in this section:

1. Construct a shingle fingerprint F_{S_j} for each document d_j, where a shingle fingerprint is a fixed-length set of hashes called shingles (see below).

---

[26]The algorithm is under standardization by the Internet Engineering Task Force: https://www.ietf.org/.
[27]Originally the method was called w-shingling. We omit the w for convenience reasons.

2. Store (in memory or on disk) for each shingle s_i and each document fingerprint F_{S_j}, such that $s_i \in F_{S_j}$, a pair $\langle s_i, U_j \rangle$, where U_j is a unique identifier of document d_j, for example the document's URL or a numeric index into a table of such URLs.

3. Sort the shingle—document identifier pairs by the shingle values.

4. Process the sorted pairs, and write new pairs of two document identifiers such that for every two shingle—document identifier pairs where $\langle s_k, U_l \rangle$ and $\langle s_k, U_m \rangle$, a pair $\langle U_l, U_m \rangle$ is created. This can be done by linearly processing the sorted pairs, because pairs with identical shingles are next to each other.

5. Sort the document identifier pairs $\langle U_l, U_m \rangle$ and count the frequency of each type of pair. The frequency of $\langle U_l, U_m \rangle$ is the number of shared shingles between d_l and d_m.

6. If the frequency of some $\langle U_l, U_m \rangle$ exceeds a certain threshold, erase one of the documents corresponding to U_l and U_m (preferably the smaller one).

The trick, informally speaking, is that we represent the document n-grams by a set which is smaller (on average) and that we massively reduce the comparison task by turning into the linear processing of a sorted list. The computationally most demanding task is the shingle creation (cf. below). The sorting processes in steps 3 and 5 can be performed efficiently using a divide—sort—merge approach, where smaller files are sorted separately and then merged in a zipper-like fashion. Even off-the-shelf tools like GNU sort apply this strategy and can be used in these cases (if text files are used to store the tuples) for hands-on implementations, and the counting in step (5) can be accomplished using GNU uniq.

For very frequent shingles, step 4 obviously creates quite a lot of pairs of document identifiers. Although it is not a sound procedure, shingles which occur in more than a certain number of documents (a threshold to be set heuristically) can be discarded completely to avoid this—at the cost of some accuracy.

Finally, how are the shingle fingerprints created? The procedure (for each document) is in fact quite simple:[28]

1. Create the set N of the document's n-grams.

2. Hash the n-grams using an i-bit hash function, forming the set H of hashes. Notice that $|N| = |H|$.

3. Permute the hashes using j (usually several hundred) random permutations of the i-bit integers, creating the sets $P_1..P_j$ of permuted hashes. Notice that $|N| = |H| = |P_n|$ for each P_n from $P_1..P_j$.

4. Take the minimum value $\min(P_n)$ from each P_n in $P_1..P_j$ and put them in the shingle fingerprint F_S. Notice that $|F_S| = j$.

The technically demanding task here is step 3, because coming up with random permutations of 64-bit integers (the recommended hash size) is not a simple task. A good solution to

---

[28]We describe the minimum hash method; cf. the referenced papers and introductions for the similar modulo hash method.

avoid this is to use Rabin hashes [Rabin, 1981]. They can be computed very efficiently, and there is a huge supply of different Rabin hash functions which can be used instead of permutations of a single hash: The Rabin hash function is seeded with a binary representation of an irreducible polynomial of degree j (for j-bit hashes), and we can thus easily create hundreds of different Rabin hash functions ad hoc. We are not aware of a Rabin hash implementation in standard libraries, but there are efficient sample implementations, for example an `ObjectPascal` implementation in our own `texrex` suite, which is based on a `Java` implementation also available with the source code under an open license.[29] Among the available all-in-one software solutions for near-duplicate removal are `texrex` and `Onion`.[30]

SUMMARY

In this chapter, we have described commonly applied techniques to cleanse raw web data from whatever might be considered undesirable corpus material: markup, boilerplate, foreign language material, duplicates. It must be kept in mind that all these techniques involve design decisions and alter the data in some way. This is especially true because we usually use computational methods which do not perfectly implement our design decisions, but introduce a certain error. This (as well as the nature of the data itself) causes problems for the subsequent processing steps (Chapter 4), but it also has to be kept in mind by corpus users. For example, if boilerplate removal was applied at the sentence, paragraph, or block level, then certain types of research require extra caution. Chapter 5 will introduce some simple and effective methods to assess the amount of some types of noise introduced by non-linguistic post-processing.

---

[29]http://sourceforge.net/projects/rabinhash/
[30]http://code.google.com/p/onion/

CHAPTER 4

Linguistic Processing

4.1 INTRODUCTION

After having applied the processing steps discussed in the previous chapters, we finally have a (possibly huge) body of clean text. In this chapter, we discuss the basics of linguistic post-processing: In order to make the web corpus a usable resource for linguistic research, the minimal processing is to split it up into word and sentence tokens. Moreover, the more levels of additional reliable linguistic annotation there are, the more useful a corpus will be. There are many different kinds of annotations, both on the word level and on the level of larger spans of text. These include part-of-speech labels and lemmas, syntactic phrase structure and dependency structure, semantic labels such as word senses or named entities, semantic/pragmatic annotation levels like co-reference, information structural labels such as topic and focus, and many more. Some corpora also include meta-data for the whole document (e.g., authorship, date of authorship, etc., genre, domain), which can also be exploited in linguistic studies. Given the size of most web corpora, tokenization as well as all other annotations have to be done automatically.

This chapter deals with the basic steps of linguistic post-processing, namely tokenization, part-of-speech tagging, and lemmatization. There is a huge number of tools freely available for these tasks, and we mention only some of them. The main purpose of this chapter is to draw attention to the typical problems that arise with the kind of noisy data specific to web corpora. Where applicable, we point out possible solutions and workarounds. Since we have optimal access to the data from diverse processing stages of our own corpora, we use them to derive examples.

Having read through this chapter, readers should:

1. have an understanding of what tokenizing, lemmatizing, and part-of-speech tagging a text usually involves,
2. have an idea of the main sources of noise in web corpora and which problems this noise causes for standard NLP tools,
3. know how the amount of some types of this noise can be reduced in relatively simple ways while being aware that other kinds of noise are much harder to fix automatically in a reliable manner.

4.2 BASICS OF TOKENIZATION, PART-OF-SPEECH TAGGING, AND LEMMATIZATION

In this section, we give an overview of the techniques used in automatic tokenization, part-of-speech tagging, and lemmatization, before we turn to the specific challenges that web corpora present in this area. Readers with a background in NLP can skip the following paragraphs and continue with Section 4.3.

4.2.1 TOKENIZATION

The raw data used to build a corpus is usually contained in one or more text files. The text consist of strings of characters, including formatting characters like newline or carriage return. In order to make it usable for most applications, it has to be broken up into smaller, linguistically meaningful units. From a linguistic perspective, the resulting tokens should be of a size such that linguistic features can be attributed to them. Minimally, these units are words and sentences. Splitting up words into smaller morphological units is also possible, although it is rarely done. Phrasal constituents (usually consisting of several words but being smaller than sentences) are of course also bearers of linguistic features, but these are much harder to detect automatically than words or sentences. Their automatic identification typically requires that the data have undergone tokenization already, along with a part-of-speech annotation for each word token. *Tokenization* usually refers to the process of dividing the input into word tokens, whereas detecting sentence boundaries is also referred to as *sentence splitting*.

In the writing systems of many languages, a word token is a string of non-whitespace characters, bounded on either side by whitespace or some punctuation mark. For instance, among the major writing systems of the world, this is true for the Cyrillic and Latin alphabets. On the other hand, a significant number of (predominantly Asian) writing systems do not explicitly mark word boundaries. As a consequence, words have to be discovered in an unlabeled stream of symbols (see Goldsmith, 2010, for a summary of commonly used techniques). Well-known examples include the Chinese ideographic script and Chinese-based syllabic scripts (Japanese Kana). Automatic tokenization of such texts is a much more challenging task that has drawn considerable attention over the last two-and-a-half decades (see overviews in Wu and Tseng, 1993; Teahan et al., 2000; Xue, 2003; Huang et al., 2007). For example, approaches to tokenizing Chinese (e. g., Chen and Liu, 1992) often involve a dictionary against which the input string is matched, and a heuristics that resolves potential ambiguities (when a string of characters can be parsed into more than one sequence of lexical items). Other approaches are purely statistical (e. g., Sproat and Shih, 1990 for Chinese; Ando and Lee, 2003 for Japanese) or combine lexico-grammatical knowledge with statistical information (e. g., Sproat et al., 1996). More recently, machine learning approaches have been proposed for this kind of task as well (see Huang et al., 2007, and references therein). In sum, then, tokenization of non-segmented languages has developed into its own sub-field of computational linguistics, which cannot be covered adequately in this introduction. In what follows, we will therefore concentrate on languages which mark word boundaries explicitly in written text.

As a first approximation, a tokenizer could split strings on whitespace and on a small number of dedicated punctuation marks, such as [. ! ?]. This simplistic approach will produce correct results in many, but not all cases. The two main reasons for this are:

- Some punctuation marks, most notably the period, are ambiguous between several functions. For example, a period can mark the end of a sentence (in which case it is a separate token), it can be part of an abbreviation (in which case it is not a separate token), it can occur as part of ordinal numbers (in which case it is not a separate token), or its function can be a combination of these (e. g., an abbreviation at the end of a sentence). The ambiguity of periods thus concerns both word tokenization and sentence splitting.
- Not every instance of a whitespace character marks a word boundary. Multi-word expressions (MWEs, words with space(s)) consist of a sequence of two or more units separated by whitespace, and because of its high degree of lexicalization, the entire sequence is considered as a single token. What exactly should count as a multi-word expression is a matter of debate and depends on linguistic considerations as well as on the particular language under investigation. English MWEs (presented here as examples to give a rough idea) arguably include constructions like compound nouns (*vice president*), fixed phrases (*by and large*), complex prepositions/adverbials (*in order to*), idioms (*bite the bullet*), phrasal verbs (*to pick up*) and named entities (*European Union*).

Many tokenizers use hand-coded rules in order to split the input into tokens. Examples of tokenizers using this technique are the Penn Treebank tokenizer [MacIntyre, 1995], Ucto [van Gompel et al., 2012], and the tokenization script that ships with the TreeTagger [Schmid, 1994b]. Tokenizers of this kind match a number of regular expressions against the input in a particular order. Some of them also perform sentence splitting. In addition, it is very common to use one or more lists of strings that should not be split any further, most notably lists of multi-word expressions and known abbreviations in a particular language (see Grefenstette and Tapanainen, 1994, for an early evaluation of different strategies for distinguishing between abbreviations and sentence boundaries). Furthermore, tokenizers of this kind usually come equipped with a heuristics in order to handle ambiguous punctuation marks. This is necessary because no list of abbreviations will ever be complete, as abbreviating words is a productive process.

On the other hand, there are also machine learning approaches to tokenization. In such approaches, regularities of punctuation are extracted automatically from text. This usually requires manually annotated training data (as in Palmer and Hearst, 1997), but unsupervised methods have been proposed as well (e. g., Kiss and Strunk, 2006; Schmid, 2000).

A primary cue for ambiguity resolution, exploited by many tokenizers (both the hand-crafted ones and the ones based on machine learning), is provided by the token which follows an ambiguous case, most notably capitalization and character class. Some tokenizers also make use of a larger context. For example, Palmer and Hearst [1997] use 3-grams on each side of a period; Mikheev [2002] extracts information from the current document; Grefenstette and Tapanainen

[1994], Kiss and Strunk [2006], and Schmid [2000] use information computed from the entire corpus.

The kind of information that tokenizers rely on also varies: word-based tokenizers may look up information about (potential) tokens in a lexicon; some sentence detectors use part-of-speech information, thus requiring labeled input data (an example is the system of Palmer and Hearst, 1997). Other systems extract various kinds of frequency information (e. g., capitalization vs. non-capitalization of the same word, Schmid, 2000; collocation measures, Kiss and Strunk, 2006) which can then be used to decide ambiguous cases.

High-quality tokenization of the data is essential for subsequent steps of linguistic post-processing, since virtually all of these steps involve reasoning about word tokens (or their annotations) in one way or another, and shortcomings in tokenization can lead to substantially increased error rates in later, higher level linguistic processing. State-of-the-art tokenizers and sentence splitters achieve a very high accuracy (some of them exceeding 99%) when tested on a manually annotated gold standard corpus. For English, it is usually a corpus like the Brown Corpus or the Wall Street Journal Corpus. For an overview of the tasks and challenges of tokenization and sentence boundary detection, see e. g., Mikheev [2003].

4.2.2   PART-OF-SPEECH TAGGING

Part-of-speech tagging (POS tagging) is the process by which each token in a corpus is assigned its part of speech. Voutilainen [2003] notes that part-of-speech tagging has been a topic of research since the late 1950s, but it was only in the late 1970s that the accuracy of such systems reached a relatively high level (around 96% of correctly classified words). Essentially, given a tokenized input text, a tagger determines the possible part-of-speech tags of a token, for example by looking them up in a lexicon. If a token is ambiguous between two or more parts of speech, the tagger must determine which POS is the correct one in the given context (disambiguation). If a token is unknown, i. e., not in the lexicon, the tagger must guess its part-of-speech tag. The information necessary for disambiguation may come from looking at the context of an ambiguous token (typically the POS tags of one or two preceding tokens), and from features of the token itself, such as the frequency with which it occurs as a particular part of speech [Manning and Schütze, 1999, Ch. 10]. Similarly, the context can be exploited to guess the part of speech of an unknown word, in combination with information of the unknown word itself, for example morphological cues such as suffixes and orthographic cues like capitalization.

A host of different techniques have been explored to tackle these tasks, including hand-crafted rules (see Voutilainen, 2003 for an introduction), rules induced by transformation learning [Brill, 1992, 1995], combinations of rules with a statistical component (e. g., Tapanainen and Voutilainen, 1994), hidden Markov models (HMMs; see Manning and Schütze, 1999 for an overview), HMMs in combination with decision trees (e. g., Schmid, 1994b), maximum entropy models (e. g., Berger et al., 1996; Ratnaparkhi, 1998), as well as machine learning approaches such as artificial neural networks (e. g., Schmid, 1994a), Conditional Random Fields (e. g., Lafferty et al., 2001), Support Vector Machines (e. g., Giménez and Màrquez, 2003), and k-nearest neighbor (e. g., van den Bosch et al., 2007).

Reported per-word accuracy of state-of-the-art taggers is usually in the range of 96–98% on standard written language, usually newspaper texts. Reported figures for some taggers even exceed 98% (e. g., Tapanainen and Voutilainen, 1994). However, these figures must be interpreted considering that up to 90% accuracy can be achieved just by always choosing the most frequent part of speech of a given token in ambiguous cases (see Church and Mercer, 1993). Thus, the baseline that taggers have to exceed is quite high to begin with. The accuracy is considerably lower for unknown words. Tagging accuracy in web data will be addressed in Section 4.5.

From a practical point of view, there are considerable differences between implemented POS taggers both in terms of processing speed and the amount of memory required. Another important difference is that while many taggers have to be trained with hand-annotated data, other taggers can also learn from raw text. Thus, when we are planning to train a tagger (instead of using one of the language models that ship with most taggers), then the choice of a particular tagger also depends on whether or not annotated training data is available. At the end of this chapter, we offer a list of suggestions for freely available NLP software.

4.2.3   LEMMATIZATION

Lemmatization is the process of reducing a set of inflected or derivationally related word forms to a smaller number of more general representations (see Fitschen and Gupta, 2008, on which much of the following paragraph is based).

A relatively simple variant of lemmatization is stemming, the process of truncating words, usually by applying some kind of heuristics. The remaining part of the word form does not in all cases correspond to a lexical item in the particular language, and the removed material may or may not correspond to derivational or inflectional morphemes (see Porter, 1980, for a classic stemming algorithm for English). More elaborate variants of lemmatization involve a lexicon and perform an analysis of a word form's morphological structure which can then be output as a morphological tag, along with a lemma. Computationally, morphological analyses are very commonly implemented using finite-state techniques (see Goldsmith, 2010, for a summary and references).

Depending on the language, a substantial proportion of word forms may be ambiguous in that they allow for more than one morphological parse. For instance, Yuret and Türe [2006] report that nearly 50% of the words in running text are morphologically ambiguous in Turkish. It is thus necessary to include a component that disambiguates between several morphological analyses of a given word form. Such disambiguation can be rule-governed or probabilistic, or a combination of these, and it may rely on additional information, such as part-of-speech tags. In practice, part-of-speech tagging and lemmatization are often performed jointly by the same piece of software.

As Fitschen and Gupta [2008] stress, the accuracy of lemmatization depends to a large extent on the quality and size of the lexicon. In case a word form cannot be mapped to one of the lemmas in the lexicon, lemmatizers follow different strategies. For example, a lemma may be marked as unknown, a lemma may be a simple copy of the word form found in the input, or the lemmatizer may try to guess a lemma on the basis of a partial morphological analysis (for instance, if a suffix could be recognized). Issues concerning the lemmatizer's lexicon are especially relevant, as web corpora tend to have a particularly large vocabulary and many items are unlikely to be listed in any lexicon for reasons to be discussed in the next section.

4.3   LINGUISTIC POST-PROCESSING OF NOISY DATA

4.3.1   INTRODUCTION

As stated above, state-of-the-art tokenizers and sentence splitters achieve a very high accuracy when tested on carefully edited, standard written language. Similarly, reported accuracy in part-of-speech tagging usually refers to performance tests on standard written language. As a matter of fact, it is often the same corpora that are used in benchmarking tokenizers and sentence splitters. However, the kind of data we are dealing with when constructing web corpora presents its own challenges for tokenizers and part-of-speech taggers, most of all because web corpora tend to contain a relatively high level of noise even after all the cleanup steps discussed in the previous chapters. Noise in web corpora includes:[1]

- faulty punctuation, in particular omitted punctuation marks or omitted whitespace after punctuation marks,
- non-standard orthography, either erroneously or as part of particular writing conventions in certain web genres, for example, ignoring standard capitalization rules or using contracted forms (like English *dunno* < *don't know*, German *haste* < *hast du* 'have you'),
- incomplete cleansing of code and HTML-markup during (non-linguistic) post-processing,
- all kinds of strings that resist straightforward tokenization and POS tagging even from a conceptual point of view, for example:

%SystemRoot%\System32
$RapperDenIchNichtKenne
$ENV{PERL5DB}
Here's-a-belt-for-the-Rat
AbCdEfGhIjKlMnOpQrStUvWxYz

But why is noise such a problem at all, given the huge size of web corpora and the fact that the vast majority of units are still tokenized and POS tagged correctly? Web corpus designers and users have to care about this because noise in the form of tokenization errors, misspellings, foreign language material, non-words, etc., leads to a very high count of lexical types, in particular hapax

---

[1]Notice that much of what must be called noise in this context might be called the relevant part of the signal in certain fields of research, such as research on non-standard spellings. The reason why we classify it as noise is that it deviates from the kind of language that most NLP tools are designed to cope with, and it therefore causes difficulties.

legomena (words that occur only once in the corpus). We will refer to types created by this kind of error as *pseudo-types*.

An immediate consequence of the presence of pseudo-types is that any figure concerning the lexicon size (number of different tokens in the corpus) will be distorted, perhaps massively so. This can reduce usability of the corpus for research questions that need to refer to the lexicon size in one way or another. Figure 4.1 illustrates this with data from the German DECOW2012 corpus (see also Liu and Curran, 2006, for similar counts in other web corpora):

N tokens:	9,108,097,177
N types:	63,569,767
N hapax legomena:	39,988,127

Figure 4.1: Proliferation of types: type and token counts for German web corpus DECOW2012.

On closer inspection, it turns out that in this specific corpus, about one half of all hapax legomena is due to the four sources of noise mentioned above (see Figure 4.2). In this particular corpus then, we have roughly 20 million pseudo-types that do not occur more than once. However, a fair number of such pseudo-types are instantiated by more than one token in a large web corpus if no measures are taken to prevent it. For example, as will be illustrated in Section 4.5, some spelling errors are quite common, thus adding to the count of pseudo-types. Thus, noise can have a huge influence on important properties of a web corpus.

Some of this noise can be reduced in the linguistic post-processing, but a certain level of noise will most likely always remain in web corpora of giga-token size, and this has to be borne in mind because it has consequences for the kind of linguistic research questions that can be answered using the final corpus.

Source	%	95% CI ($\pm$%)
misspelling	20.0	5.0
tokenization error	17.6	4.7
non-word	7.6	3.3
foreign-language material	6.8	3.1
rare word	46.8	6.2
number	1.2	1.3

Figure 4.2: Noise in web corpora: classification of hapax legomena (DECOW2012). Estimated proportions of different categories ($n = 250$), with 95% confidence interval (CI).

4.3.2   TREATMENT OF NOISY DATA

In the context of natural language processing, the handling of noisy data has attracted an increasing number of researchers in recent years due to the ever-growing amount of text available from noisy web sources (as in informal text types like emails, chat protocols, blogs, forums, tweets, etc.), and this is reflected in a growing body of literature on the subject. Some of the noise problems we find in web corpora, e. g., the omission of whitespace, are comparable to those encountered with texts obtained from OCR'd (optical character recognition) sources (cf. Esakov et al., 1994; Lopresti, 2009). Other problems, such as the omission of punctuation marks, are reminiscent of tokenization/sentence splitting of data obtained from automatic speech recognition, where orthographic end-of-sentence markers are missing altogether and sentence boundaries must be inferred using other cues [Ostendorf et al., 2007]. Still other problems, like misspellings, have also attracted attention in other areas of Computational Linguistics, such as text mining, term extraction, ontology building, information retrieval, and query optimization. For an overview of classical techniques for spelling correction, see Kukich [1992]. For a more recent survey on different aspects of the noise problem in natural language processing, and techniques for dealing with it, see e. g., Subramaniam et al. [2009] and the references in Section 4.6 below.

However, to the best of our knowledge, the applicability of such techniques in the creation of web corpora has not been evaluated yet. Hence, it is an open question whether they can be exploited for normalizing web corpora.[2] The principal challenge, as we see it, is that constructing a resource suitable for linguistic research requires a very high degree of precision. If in doubt, it is better to leave the data unchanged than to apply inadequate normalizations. As a consequence, rather than proposing a general solution to the noise problem in the linguistic post-processing of web corpora, we will illustrate the kind of problems that typically arise when tokenizing, lemmatizing, and part-of-speech tagging noisy web texts, and show how some of them can be overcome (or at least, reduced) by applying a number of simple measures. These are intended to give the reader a rough idea of the kind of pre-processing that may be required. In any case, anyone building a web corpus needs to inspect their data, detect potential problems, and find a suitable solution. In Section 4.4, we illustrate the usefulness of applying some simple but efficient pre-processing steps before tokenizing noisy web data by two examples: omitted whitespace after sentence-ending punctuation and emoticons.

4.4   TOKENIZING WEB TEXTS

4.4.1   EXAMPLE: MISSING WHITESPACE

Consider the omission of whitespace after end-of-sentence punctuation. Token-internal periods, as exemplified with data from the British National Corpus in Figure 4.3, are not much of an issue when tokenizing standard written language because erroneous omissions of whitespace after an end-of-sentence period are relatively rare (cf. Schmid, 2000, 14 for a similar assumption).[3] However, such omissions are more frequent in the informal text types that are likely to populate

---

[2]Some sparse remarks are found, e. g., in Fletcher [2011], but without mentioning concrete web corpus projects which have applied spell-checking.
[3]But this is not to say that the problem is nonexistent with standard written language: there are also instances of erroneously omitted whitespace after punctuation in various sections of the BNC, similar to those in Fig. 4.4.

web corpora. Figure 4.4 illustrates this with data from the English UKCOW2012 corpus (ca. 6 billion tokens).

Token(s)	Original Context
12.6.1986	The Daily Telegraph, **12.6.1986**
340p.p.m.	these small vein zircons are U-rich (average **340p.p.m.**)
$2.1m 41.8m	mid-term net losses stood at **$2.1m** up from losses of **41.8m** last time
$2.1m	Performances start at **7.30pm** Wednesday-Saturday

Figure 4.3: Examples of token-internal periods in "standard" text (BNC): can be ignored by tokenizer/sentence splitter.

Token	Original Context
part.There	I have played a very modest **part.There** are a whole lot of people who
cloth.There	eg with a dry linen or cotton **cloth.There** are all sorts of peg pastes w
reason.If	lding you back for a specific **reason.If** we are honest, our equipment
quarry.You	uising slowly looking for our **quarry.You** are in the most superb wilder
otters.You	mentioned so far is the giant **otters.You** may have seen these on TV as
weeks.We	sed in this action-packed two **weeks.We** have been fortunate enough to

Figure 4.4: Omitted whitespace after punctuation. The first column shows the token that would result if no splitting on the token-internal period were performed. The second column shows some of the context in which the token appears in the corpus.

One possibility to handle this problem is to separate these so-called *run-ons* before passing the text to the tokenizer. A simple regular expression that singles out (a subset of) the problematic cases is given here:

```
[:alpha:]\{2,\}[.?!;:,][:upper:][:lower:]\+
```

A tool like GNU sed could be used to insert a whitespace character after the punctuation mark. It may take a few trials until the best strategy for a particular task is found, and it is a good idea to evaluate the effect of such substitutions on a sample before processing the entire corpus. For example, substitutions based on the above regular expression had a precision of 94.3% ($\pm 2.9\%$ at a 95% confidence level). That is, 94.3% of the substitutions affected the sort of orthographic irregularity they were supposed to, but there were also a few false positives (mainly URLs containing capital letters). Other regular expressions could have matched more run-ons, for example instances where the second word includes punctuation marks (such as the apostrophe in *ok.You'll*) or does not start with a capital letter (new sentences starting with a lower-case letter are occasionally found in informal writing), or where whitespace is missing not after [.?!;:,], but rather after a quotation mark or a closing parenthesis (as in *ok."You*). Extending the above regular expression to match such cases would likely raise the recall (i. e., match more run-ons), but almost certainly at the cost of lower precision (i. e., more matched strings which are not run-ons) if no further measures are taken.

One way of achieving a higher precision is to perform a lexicon look-up for the two putative words at either side of the putatively missing whitespace, and only insert a whitespace if both are found in the lexicon. For example, using GNU Aspell's British English lexicon, along with a slightly more complicated regular expression covering all the additional cases just mentioned, we obtained not a single false positive in experiments on the UKCOW2012 corpus.[4] Alternatively, a domain-specific lexicon can be bootstrapped from the corpus during a first pass and look-ups can then be performed with that lexicon. Another option is to check during a first pass whether the second putative word is a frequent sentence starter in the corpus, and use this information during a second pass for deciding whether or not a whitespace should be inserted [Schmid, 2008].

Thus, using simple substitutions before tokenization, instances of non-standard punctuation (and other irregularities) can be fixed that would otherwise result in pseudo tokens (increasing the number of hapax legomena), and get in the way of proper sentence boundary detection. In addition, a few lines of code written in a script language around a regular expression are sufficient to considerably enhance the quality of such substitutions, e. g., by checking strings against a lexicon or by computing frequencies of occurrence.

4.4.2   EXAMPLE: EMOTICONS

Another characteristic of many texts obtained from the web is the widespread use of emoticons of all kinds, like those illustrated in Figures 4.5 and 4.6. Emoticons do not normally appear in newspaper texts or other texts written in a more formal register. Thus, any tokenizer designed for such kinds of text will likely split emoticons into their component parts if no measures are taken to prevent this. For example, the Penn Treebank tokenizer would split them up, as well as the TreeTagger tokenizer. However, at least in our view, emoticons should be preserved in the final corpus, not only because splitting them up means distorting the frequency of their component parts, but also because they are a unique feature of certain genres of electronic communication and constitute a topic of investigation in their own right. So, if emoticons should be preserved for the final corpus, the tokenizer must be modified in a way that it does not split them into their component parts. With rule-based tokenizers, this can easily be achieved by adding one or more rules, e. g., in the form of regular expressions that match emoticons, or as a list of strings that must not be split. In our experience, a combination of these works well. For example, in the Dutch web corpus NLCOW2012 (total: 2.36 billion tokens), we recognized a total of almost 400,000 emoticons using this simple method.

:)   ;)   ;-)   :D   ;D   :)))   :P

Figure 4.5: Normal ASCII smileys (conveniently also referred to here as emoticons).

---

[4]http://aspell.net/

```
:wink:   :rolleyes:   :lol:   :confused:   :mrgreen:   :angel:   :cool:
```

Figure 4.6: Emoticons in the markdown syntax of the popular forum software `phpBB` (usually rendered as images on the actual web page).

4.5   POS TAGGING AND LEMMATIZATION OF WEB TEXTS

POS taggers that were trained on standard written language and which are reported to deliver high accuracy on this kind of data, are normally not as good at handling web texts. Giesbrecht and Evert [2009] study the performance of several popular and freely available state-of-the-art POS taggers: TnT [Brants, 2000], `TreeTagger` [Schmid, 1995], `UIMA` Tagger, `SVMTool` [Giménez and Màrquez, 2004] and the `Stanford Tagger` [Toutanova et al., 2003].[5,6] All taggers were trained on the same corpus of German newspaper texts (TIGER; Brants et al., 2002). Giesbrecht and Evert find that all taggers fall short of reaching the high level of accuracy reported in the respective publications, even in tagging standard newspaper texts. The performance on web data is still lower, but varies with the genre of the text. For all taggers, the lowest accuracy (between 79.97% and 88.01%) is achieved in tagging texts from online forums. This is to be expected, since the language used in many web forums is indeed informal and differs quite dramatically from carefully edited newspaper text. In terms of overall accuracy on web data, `TreeTagger` (using the pre-packaged parameter file) outperforms the other taggers (at 94.77% accuracy). The authors also report that the ratio of unknown words is substantially higher in web corpora than in newspaper corpora. Since for all tested taggers, per-word accuracy is better with known words than with unknown words, they identify the relatively large vocabulary of web corpora as one the sources of low tagger performance. As we will show below, and in line with the findings of Giesbrecht and Evert [2009], the principal challenges in part-of-speech tagging of web texts are:

- noise, mostly in the form of non-standard orthography, both intentional (genre-specific writing conventions) and unintentional (spelling errors), as well as foreign language material,
- lexical characteristics of web texts (domain terms).

In order to enhance tagging accuracy of web texts, we need an idea of how much impact each one of these factors has. In the following section, we illustrate this.

4.5.1   TRACING BACK ERRORS IN POS TAGGING

As a first example, consider the data in Figure 4.7, taken from the English UKCOW2011 corpus (0.9 billion tokens). The corpus was POS tagged with `TreeTagger` using the standard English parameter file. In Figure 4.7, we list the top 60 word forms that were unknown to the tagger. Among the unknown word forms, there are newly coined terms, colloquial and genre-specific

---

[5]`http://uima.apache.org/downloads/sandbox/hmmTaggerUsersGuide/hmmTaggerUsersGuide.html`
[6]`http://www.lsi.upc.edu/~nlp/SVMTool/`

expressions (like *website, blog, url*), cases of non-standard or faulty orthography (*dont, thats*), as well as word forms that could not be found in the lexicon because the input was not tokenized correctly (*and/, days., 'The*). Many of the unknown forms are assigned a correct part-of-speech tag because the tagger guessed it successfully from the context, such as *website, blog, healthcare*. Others are probably classified incorrectly, e. g., *Regulations* is tagged as a proper noun, and *F1* as an adjective. Notice also how the tagger interprets capitalization of a word as evidence for a classification as proper noun, even if it knows the word in its non-capitalized form.

Rank	Word form	POS tag	Rank	Word form	POS tag	Rank	Word form	POS tag
1	website	NN	21	Ofcom	NP	41	Advice	NP
2	email	NN	22	HMRC	NP	42	Equality	NP
3	blog	NN	23	download	VB	43	Panel	NP
4	url	NN	24	dont	VBP	44	'I	NNS
5	Boro	NP	25	blogs	NNS	45	Schedule	NP
6	Devil	NP	26	Tribunal	NP	46	Facebook	NP
7	Google	NP	27	e-mail	NP	47	Awards	NP
8	and/	NN	28	Practice	NP	48	Higher	NP
9	Blog	NP	29	days.	NN	49	emails	NNS
10	Blogger	NP	30	Online	NP	50	Lottery	NP
11	Library	NP	31	MPA	NP	51	Primary	NP
12	websites	NNS	32	Regulations	NP	52	F1	JJ
13	Programme	NP	33	dont	NN	53	Syndrome	NP
14	Support	NP	34	Award	NP	54	NOT	NP
15	broadband	NN	35	Twitter	NP	55	Teaching	NP
16	Windows	NP	36	eg	NN	56	'The	JJ
17	Scheme	NP	37	iPhone	NN	57	Ombudsman	NP
18	healthcare	NN	38	apps	NNS	58	email	VB
19	carers	NNS	39	3D	JJ	59	thats	NNS
20	download	NN	40	Linux	NP	60	Directory	NP

Figure 4.7: Top 60 word forms of UKCOW2011 that are not in `TreeTagger`'s lexicon (standard English parameter file, using the Penn Treebank tagset).

So, while the `TreeTagger` lexicon lacked quite a number of words, the tagger was able to make correct guesses for a considerable number of unknown word forms. It is instructive to look at the sources of unknown words to get a better overview of which should count as noise and which should count as data, especially in documents which contain a high amount of informal language. We identified those documents in the DECOW2012 corpus (most of them forum discussions and blog entries), using a simple heuristic as suggested in Schäfer and Sayatz (submitted).[7] For the resulting sub-corpus ($N \approx 1.9$ billion tokens), it is expected that a standard POS tagger delivers particularly low accuracy. The texts were processed with `TreeTagger`, using the German standard parameter file and no additional lexicon. Words unknown to the tagger were extracted along with the POS tag which the tagger had assigned to them. For the 1,000 most frequent word-POS combinations, the tagger reached only 26.3% overall accuracy. The cases in which the tagger

---

[7]I. e., we looked for occurrences of the short forms of the German indefinite article, such as *nem, ne, ner*, which are highly indicative of informal writing.

did not assign the correct POS tag were manually classified, the results of which are shown in Figure 4.8.

Class	%
non-standard orthography	32.3
lexicon gaps	19.8
foreign language material	18.9
emoticons	13.7
named entities	5.4
tokenization errors	3.1
other	6.8

Figure 4.8: Classification of errors in POS tagging for a sub-corpus of informal language from the German DECOW2012.

The main source of unknown word forms (in this portion of the corpus) is non-standard orthography, and we do not expect such forms to be part of the lexicon of a standard POS tagger. The second most important category is words that are not in the tagger's lexicon although they are spelled correctly. About 50% of them are domain terms, and another 40% are abbreviations. Foreign-language material also has its fair share in causing tagging errors.[8] Emoticons constitute another and relatively important class. Named entities, tokenization errors, and all other sources taken together make up for the rest of unknown words. Taking a closer look at the cases of non-standard orthography, we see that it comprises a number of quite different cases, as shown in Figure 4.9, examples of which are given in Figure 4.10.

Class	%
genre-specific spellings	59.2
omitted whitespace	13.4
variants	19.7
ordinary typos	7.56

Figure 4.9: Breakdown of non-standard orthography in informal language of DECOW2012.

Genre-specific spellings are intentional deviations from standard orthography. In typical cases, informal spoken language is imitated, including contractions of finite verbs, prepositions or conjunctions with a following pronoun or article, dropped characters, and orthographical renderings of dialectal pronunciations. Most cases of omitted whitespace are probably also intentional genre-specific spellings, but some could also be plain typos. Variants are spellings where the non-ASCII characters *ä, ö, ü, ß* are replaced with the ASCII-compatible alternative strings *ae, oe, ue,*

---

[8]Note that the distinction between domain terms and foreign-language material is not always straightforward, as German and many other languages borrow much of their specialized vocabulary from English.

ss, respectively, as well as words that differ from their standard spelling only in case, e. g., nouns starting with a lower case letter, or adverbs starting with an upper case letter. Strictly speaking, not all of these are even cases of non-standard orthography. The tagger sometimes just failed to recognize sentence-initial occurences of words which are usually written in lower case sentence-internally. Finally, there are also unintentional orthographic errors, including purely typographic errors and cognitive errors (due to ignorance of the standard orthography; see Kukich, 1992).

non-standard	standard	translation		non-standard	standard	translation
GENRE-SPECIFIC ORTHOGRAPHY				VARIANTS		
finds	finde es	'find it'		*fuer*	für	'for'
weils	weil es	'because it'		*koennte*	könnte	'could'
aufn	auf den	'on the'		*leute*	Leute	'people'
gesehn	gesehen	'seen'		*Hatte*	(sent. init.)	'had'
geb	gebe	'(I) give'		*Vielen*	(sent. init.)	'much/many'
ned	nicht	'not'		ORDINARY TYPOS		
bissl	bisschen	'some'		*nciht*	nicht	'not'
MISSING WHITESPACE				*cih*	ich	'I'
schonmal	schon mal	'ever'		*ziehmlich*	ziemlich	'quite'
Vorallem	Vor allem	'predominantly'		*vieleicht*	vielleicht	'maybe'

Figure 4.10: Non-standard spellings (examples from DECOW2012).

Now, the point of going this far into the details of incorrectly tagged unknown words is that we need to find ways of reducing these errors. It turns out that a number of simple measures are suitable to reduce the impact of some sources of error:

1. Extending the tagger's lexicon with domain terms. A list of candidate terms can be generated from the web corpus by looking for words the tagger did not know. This means that a previous step of POS tagging is necessary. Sort by descending frequency and annotate a few thousand by hand. This will not solve the problem completely, but it is likely to substantially enhance the tagger's lexical coverage on web data. Methods have been proposed for semi-automatically extending a lexicon with domain terms. For example, in the context of automatic spelling correction, Bloem et al. [2012] report that their approach of automatically adding unknown words that occur a certain number of times works well for individual, closely delineated domains. It is unclear, however, if this method is applicable to very large corpora covering a multitude of different domains. Also, the gain in lexical coverage must be balanced against the risk that a misspelled word accidentally coincides with another valid word form if the lexicon is very large [Peterson, 1986], which in turn could lead to an overall decrease in tagging accuracy.

2. Extending the lexicon with genre-specific spellings. Adding non-standard orthography to the tagger's lexicon is perfectly justifiable in building web corpora. The procedure would be the same as in 1, but this step might involve modifying the tagset as well. For example, neither the Penn tagset for English [Marcus et al., 1993] nor the STTS-tagset for German

[Schiller et al., 1999] provide compound tags for contracted forms such as *I'm*, *wanna*, *gonna*, or German *kannste* (standard: *kannst du* 'can you') etc. Note that some taggers will not allow you to use POS tags that were not included in their training data.

3. Extending the lexicon with emoticons. This is an obvious step, too, but care must be taken not to split emoticons when tokenizing the text (see Section 4.4.2). However, people might also use emoticons to stand in for words of diverse parts of speech, such that a single special tag for emoticons might also be inadequate for some cases.

4. Simplifying the tagset. Giesbrecht and Evert [2009] show how a simpler tagset reduces the error rate when tagging web data.

5. Retraining the tagger on web data. This is probably the most time consuming solution, as many POS taggers require annotated training data.

Unknown words have a major impact not only on the performance of part-of-speech taggers, but also on the accuracy of lexicon-based lemmatizers. Since the vocabulary of a web corpus is usually very large and tends to include all kinds of rare domain words, non-words, and words written with non-standard spelling, lemmatization of web corpora is a challenge similar to part-of-speech tagging. While the measures listed above are meant to increase the accuracy of POS tagging, at least some of them seem also suitable to improve the results of lemmatization. In addition to these steps, it is worthwhile to consider orthographic normalization as an additional pre-processing measure that will likely have a positive effect on the outcome of both lemmatization and part-of-speech tagging.

4.6   ORTHOGRAPHIC NORMALIZATION

Dealing with true orthographic errors is a delicate issue, both in terms of technical implementation and in terms of corpus design. It is certainly not an option to include all (or a substantial number of) typos in the tagger's lexicon, along with the POS tag and lemma of the intended word. As illustrated in Figure 4.11 with the German verb *übernimmt* ('takes over'), a large web corpus easily contains dozens of different misspellings of the same word, and many of them are not hapax legomena.

A more promising approach is orthographical normalization of non-standard spellings before POS tagging. Automatic spelling error detection and correction has been studied since the 1960s. Kukich [1992] offers a survey on the development of the discipline from its beginnings to the 1990s. More recent approaches include Ahmad and Kondrak, 2005; Cucerzan and Brill, 2004; Li et al., 2006. While simple detection of orthographic errors resulting in non-words is a relatively straightforward task (which can be performed, e. g., on the basis of character n-grams or by lexicon look-up) and can be done by just considering the misspelled word in isolation, other types of errors (primarily those which result in another correct word of the same language) are harder to detect and usually require looking at some context and linguistic features.

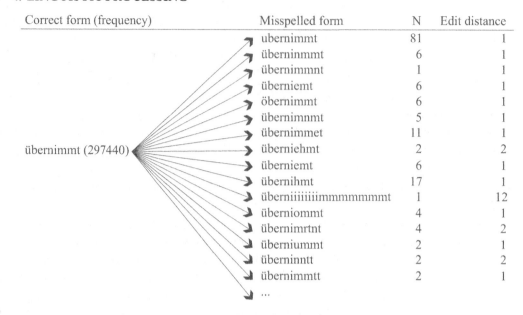

Correct form (frequency)	Misspelled form	N	Edit distance
	ubernimmt	81	1
	überninmmt	6	1
	übernimmnt	1	1
	überniemt	6	1
	öbernimmt	6	1
	übernimnmt	5	1
	übernimmet	11	1
übernimmt (297440)	überniehmt	2	2
	überniemt	6	1
	übernihmt	17	1
	überniiiiiiiiiimmmmmmmmt	1	12
	überniommt	4	1
	übernimrtnt	4	2
	überniummt	2	1
	überninntt	2	2
	übernimmtt	2	1
	...		

Figure 4.11: Some spelling variants of German *übernimmt* ('takes over') from DECOW2012. Almost all misspellings are within one deletion/insertion/substitution of distance from the correct spelling.

Going beyond mere detection of misspelled words and trying to replace them by correct forms makes the task harder as well. Usually, spellcheckers suggest a list of possible substitutions from a lexicon and rank them based on similarity with the misspelled word. One popular similarity measure is the edit distance between the misspelled form and the candidate form, which is defined as the minimal number of character insertions, deletions, substitutions, and transpositions necessary to transform one string into the other [Damerau, 1964; Levenshtein, 1966]. Empirical studies on spelling errors suggest that the majority of misspelled words is no further than one edit distance from the intended word. Reported ratios are in the range of approx. 70–95%, but these figures arguably depend to a large extent on the type of application (see Kukich, 1992). Another popular technique is to map each word to a similarity key such that phonetically similar words receive identical or similar keys (Odell and Russell, 1918; Philips, 1990; Postel, 1969, and others) and then measure the edit distance on the keys.

Still more demanding is the task of non-interactive, automatic spelling correction, where, in addition to generating a list of substitution candidates, exactly one of them must be selected to replace the misspelled word in the text. Edit distance alone is of little help here because often more than one substitution candidate has the minimal edit distance to the misspelled word. As an example, consider the misspelled word *tru* in an English text. Correction candidates (as returned by GNU Aspell) include *true* and *try*, but both are at the same edit distance (= 1) from *tru*. Attempts have been made at making a decision on the basis of other features that can be computed by considering the misspelled word in isolation, such as weighting of the different edit operations, or weighting according to the individual characters involved in an edit operation, giving less weight to more typical/more frequent spelling errors. A number of approaches take into account some of the context surrounding the misspelled word, e. g., in the form of word n-grams or POS tag n-grams, in order to select a substitution word from among several candidates. Moreover, context information on the level of the document, the entire corpus and other corpora (both general and domain specific) can be exploited for assessing the appropriateness of a substitution candidate, for example, by ranking up candidates that are likely to occur in texts of a specific domain (see e. g., Wong et al., 2007, for a recent proposal to combine information from various sources in selecting a candidate). Finally, normalizing noisy texts may also involve such things as expanding abbreviations, restoring improper casing and correcting tokenization errors, and a number of approaches and tools have been proposed to tackle this task (see e. g., Clark, 2003; Clark and Araki, 2011; Sproat et al., 2001; Wong et al., 2007).

The upshot of this is that automatic spelling correction uses heuristics and does not necessarily achieve 100% accuracy, and this is an important aspect when we want to treat texts that are going to be used in linguistic research. Perhaps most importantly, care must be taken not to normalize rare words that are unlikely to be listed in a spellchecker's dictionary (cf. the high count of rare but regular words among the hapax legomena in Figure 4.2). Discussing normalization methods in detail is beyond the scope of this introduction, but applying them in web corpus construction and evaluating the results is clearly a topic of future research.

From a linguistic perspective, it is desirable that text normalization is done in a non-destructive way, wherever this is possible, that is, leaving the original text intact. The advantage is that users of the final corpus do not have to rely on the imperfect results of, for example, automatic spelling correction. Instead, users are free to access (and base their research on) the original, non-normalized data, which can be crucial in some circumstances. Non-destructive normalization can be done by regarding the normalized forms of tokens as an additional annotation layer. Other automatic annotation tools (such as a POS tagger and a lemmatizer) can then be run on this layer to produce yet other annotation layers (e. g., the part of speech information of the corrected tokens). Figure 4.12 illustrates this with data from UKCOW2011. As a major disadvantage, this increases (potentially doubles) the size of the final corpus.

That said, the amount of time and effort necessary for cleaning and normalizing a web corpus must be balanced against the usefulness of such measures when it comes to working with the final corpus. Applying some cleaning and normalization is probably a good idea when building a corpus that will be used by more than a handful of people and is intended for research on a greater number of research questions, but the situation may be different if the goal is constructing an ad hoc corpus for a closely delimited task where exact type/token counts or accurate POS tagging are not essential. Thus, the decision about what degree of normalization is appropriate is an individual one.

Word	POS	Lemma	Corr.Word	Corr.POS	Corr.Lemma
...			...		
the	DT	the	the	DT	the
players	NNS	player	players	NNS	player
play	VBP	play	play	VBP	play
.	SENT	.	.	SENT	.
The	DT	the	The	DT	the
FA	NP	FA	FA	NP	FA
does	VBZ	do	does	VBZ	do
abosolutley	**JJ**	**\<unknown\>**	**absolutely**	**RB**	**absolutely**
nothing	NN	nothing	nothing	NN	nothing
to	TO	to	to	TO	to
help	VB	help	help	VB	help
Clubs	NNS	club	Clubs	NNS	club
,	,	,	,	,	,
...			...		

Figure 4.12: Non-destructive text normalization using annotation layers (vertical text, as suitable for processing with corpus query engines).

4.7   SOFTWARE FOR LINGUISTIC POST-PROCESSING

There are a lot of tools for linguistic processing around. Given the nature of the data and the size of giga-token web corpora (in the range of tens of gigabytes of data), a few considerations should be kept in mind when choosing a linguistic post-processing tool. The evaluation of these tools is based mostly on our own experience with them. This is not intended as an exhaustive list of appropriate software packages, which would be beyond the scope of this book.

1. Availability: Whether a package is free and/or open source will probably play a role in many academic contexts. Likewise, individuals might not be in a position to pay a substantial amount of money for NLP software.

2. Resources: A number of tools come suitably configured and will work (more or less) out-of-the-box for the kind of data we are concerned with. For example, some tools include larger numbers of language models, while others may require users to train such models on their own data.

3. Performance: Processing time and accuracy have to be balanced against each other. In the context of web corpus construction, the usually huge amounts of data make it necessary to consider this issue carefully as there are huge differences in time performance between, for example, different taggers. This may be less of an issue when a large and high quality corpus is built that will be archived and re-used for a relatively long period of time by many people. In such a case, waiting several weeks for a tagger to finish is an acceptable investment. On the other hand, if the goal is to quickly create an ad hoc web corpus for a special, restricted purpose, any post-processing task that takes more than a few days may be unacceptable.

One way to deal with this problem is parallelization of individual tasks, which usually reduces processing time by a substantial factor. A very simple solution that does not require any complicated setups and configurations is GNU Parallel, which takes care of splitting the input file into chunks, runs independent processes (e. g., taggers) on them, and joins the output from these processes in the correct order.[9] More advanced options for parallel processing include frameworks like Apache Hadoop allowing Map-Reduce operations on many machines.[10] However, the effort and time of setting up such a solution (let alone the cost of buying a cluster of machines) do not always stand in an optimal relationship with the gain in processing time, at least not when the goal is creating only a single web corpus.

That said, some tools are:

- TreeTagger [Schmid, 1995] is a very fast and very popular HMM tagger that also performs lemmatization.[11] Models are available for quite a number of languages, but (as of mid-2013) none of them are trained on web texts. It was used to process the WaCky corpora and some of the COW corpora.
- RFTagger is a POS tagger and morphological analyzer designed for fine-grained part-of-speech tagsets.[12] It ships with models for German, Czech, Slovene, and Hungarian.
- FreeLing [Padró and Stanilovsky, 2012] is a suite of NLP tools with dictionaries and models for a number of Romance languages plus English, Russian, and Welsh.[13] It is not as fast as TreeTagger, but processing speed is still acceptable even for very large corpora.
- The Stanford Tagger [Toutanova et al., 2003] is a maximum entropy tagger for which reported accuracy on standard written language is quite high.[14] In an experiment on tagging web data [Giesbrecht and Evert, 2009], it was outperformed by TreeTagger when trained on standard written texts, both in accuracy and in computing time. In addition, depending on the language model, RAM requirements can easily exceed 8G. Interestingly, it ships with a model trained on the deWaC web corpus, but to our knowledge, performance on web data has not yet been re-evaluated using this model.
- Frog [van den Bosch et al., 2007] is a memory based (k-nearest neighbor) tagger/morphological analyzer with high reported accuracy.[15] It also includes a chunker, a dependency parser, and a named entity recognizer. In our experiments, it does not compare favorably with, e. g., TreeTagger in terms of efficiency, even when used only for POS tagging.

---

[9]http://www.gnu.org/software/parallel/
[10]http://hadoop.apache.org/
[11]http://www.cis.uni-muenchen.de/~schmid/tools/TreeTagger/
[12]http://www.cis.uni-muenchen.de/~schmid/tools/RFTagger/
[13]http://nlp.lsi.upc.edu/freeling/
[14]http://www-nlp.stanford.edu/software/tagger.shtml
[15]http://ilk.uvt.nl/frog/

- Ucto [van Gompel et al., 2012] tokenizes Unicode text using hand-written rules (ordered regular expressions, supporting unicode character classes).[16] It is included as part of the Frog processing chain, but can also be used as a stand-alone application. Ucto ships with a set of configuration files for various languages and is easily adaptable to suit specific needs.
- splitta [Gillick, 2009] offers statistical sentence boundary detection using a Naive Bayes classifier or, alternatively, a Support Vector Machine.[17] As of 2013, the distribution provides models for English trained on standard written language (Wall Street Journal corpus and Brown corpus). Training routines are included to build models for languages other than English.
- NLTK [Bird et al., 2009] is a collection of Python modules, covering many different aspects of NLP such as tokenization, POS tagging, parsing, named entity recognition, etc.[18]
- Apache OpenNLP is a software suite covering several tasks in natural language processing, including tokenization, sentence boundary detection, POS tagging, chunking, parsing, named entity recognition, and document classification.[19]

SUMMARY

In this chapter, we have discussed and illustrated the primary steps of the linguistic post-processing and normalization of web data (tokenization, sentence boundary detection, POS tagging, lemmatization). It should have become clear that web documents contain various types of noise which make these steps difficult and lead to an accuracy which is measurably lower than for traditionally compiled corpora. The result is, for example, that certain counts derived from the corpus have to be treated with care (like type and token counts). Since there is no general recipe for cleaning web corpora, we illustrated some of the steps which can be taken to improve the overall quality of the linguistic post-processing. However, the main conceptual problem concerns the distinction between noise and data. Each normalization alters the data and might introduce new or even more noise, depending on the definition of noise. All this makes some form of quality control necessary. In the next chapter, we sketch some ways of how the quality and composition of web corpora can be assessed.

---

[16]http://ilk.uvt.nl/ucto/
[17]http://code.google.com/p/splitta/
[18]http://nltk.org/
[19]http://opennlp.apache.org/

CHAPTER 5

Corpus Evaluation and Comparison

5.1 INTRODUCTION

This chapter deals with ways to evaluate the quality of a web corpus. In Section 5.2, we show how to assess the overall technical quality of the corpus, suggesting a number of procedures appropriate to reveal potential shortcomings in crawling and post-processing (most notably boilerplate removal and duplicate detection), but also flaws in the general cleanup and linguistic post processing. However, the fact that a web corpus is acceptable from a technical point of view does not tell us much about the characteristics of the language and documents contained in it, and how it compares to other corpora in this respect. For example, one might be interested in the similarity of the web corpus to corpora that have known characteristics and which are established, widely used resources in the Corpus Linguistics community (sometimes called *reference corpora*). To this end, Section 5.3 takes a quantitative perspective on corpus comparison and introduces various measures of corpus similarity. Section 5.4 is dedicated to the comparison of keywords extracted from corpora in a variety of ways, thus concentrating on the topics/domains covered by the corpora. Another way of evaluating a web corpus, sometimes called *extrinsic evaluation*, is to look at it it from the perspective of specific linguistic uses of the corpus, possibly in comparison to traditional corpora. A short overview of such approaches will be given in Section 5.5. Finally, Section 5.6 briefly addresses corpus composition (in terms of text types, genres, authorship, etc.) and the questions of representativeness and balance.

Having read through this chapter, readers should:

1. know a few measures that can be used to assess the technical quality of their corpus (success of cleansing, deduplication etc.),
2. be familiar with a variety of different ways in which corpora can be evaluated, including measuring similarity between corpora, content-oriented comparison with extracted keywords, task-specific evaluation, and assessment of corpus composition,
3. be aware of the limitations of their corpus in terms of balance and representativeness.

5.2 ROUGH QUALITY CHECK

As a first step in evaluating a new web corpus, it is advisable to inspect it for obvious flaws in the processing chain. Such shortcomings include (massive) failure in removing pieces of boilerplate, duplicate documents (or parts of them) that have gone undetected, and systematic flaws in tokenization. A technique that allows for quick assessment of these aspects is computing a number of statistics from the corpus data and checking whether the distribution of the values is plausible. If it is not, a detailed inspection is necessary. In case the detected anomalies point to serious shortcomings in post-processing, it might even be necessary to redo the processing step which caused the problem. Depending on the software used in processing the raw data, a few changes in the parameter settings might be sufficient to fix the problem. More often than not, there are issues particular to a given corpus, calling for an iterative approach in constructing the final corpus. In this section, we will illustrate a rough quality check by looking at the distribution of word and sentence lengths as well as duplicated sentences.

5.2.1   WORD AND SENTENCE LENGTHS

A number of statistics can be computed in order to assess the technical quality of a web corpus. For example, there are over 200 statistics available for some of the corpora in the Leipzig Corpora Collection [Biemann et al., 2007; Goldhahn et al., 2012], many of which could be exploited for the purpose of quality control.[1] We will concentrate here on the distribution of word length and sentence length, because they are easy to compute and they have turned out to be particularly helpful in detecting anomalies in the corpus [Eckart et al., 2012].

Research on the distribution of word length has a tradition dating back over a hundred years. A good entry point to the subject is Grzybek [2007]. Mathematical modeling of empirical word length distributions depends on factors such as text type, unit of measurement (letters vs. phonemes, syllables vs. morphemes), and even on individual authors. A variety of theoretical distributions have been proposed for modeling word length, including the geometric, the log-normal, the negative binomial, the Hyper-Pascal, and, very prominently, the Poisson distribution with several generalizations (including Conway-Maxwell-Poisson and Hyper-Poisson) and variants (e. g., positive Poisson, Cohen Poisson). Several of these, such as the log-normal, the negative binomial, the Hyper-Pascal and some of the Poisson family of distributions have also been explored in modeling sentence length. As in the case of word length, the unit of measurement (e. g., number of words vs. number of clauses) plays a crucial role in choosing an appropriate theoretical distribution (see Best, 2001, 2005, for a compact overview).

Successful modeling of word and sentence length is usually based on texts written by a single author (or even only parts of such texts), and the findings do not necessarily generalize to a collection of wildly different genres written by a multitude of authors, i. e., web corpora.[2] For this reason, our rough quality check does not involve fitting a model to the data and drawing conclusions from the goodness-of-fit. Rather, massive anomalies in the distribution can be detected by visual inspection of the plotted data, and it is sufficient to assume as a rule of thumb that both

---

[1]http://cls.informatik.uni-leipzig.de/

[2]Some authors even exclude this possibility altogether, cf. Grzybek [2007, 18]: "any combination of different texts turns out to be a 'quasi-text', destroying the internal rules of text self-regulation. The very same, of course, has to be said about corpus analyses, since a corpus, from this point of view, is nothing but a quasi text."

word length and sentence length follow a positively skewed distribution, i. e., a distribution with an early mode and an extended tail of low frequencies as word/sentence length increases.

Figure 5.1 shows the distribution of word lengths, measured in number of characters, in a sample of the German DECOW2012 corpus ($n = 14.8$ million tokens). By what we can tell from the plot, the overall shape is fine. The most frequently occurring word length is 3. It is a good idea to take a quick look at the frequency list of such words to make sure this is not an artifact of post-processing. Figure 5.2 shows the frequency list of words of length 3 in the sample from DECOW2012. Of the 20 most frequent items, 19 are regular German function words and one is the ellipsis (…). There is thus no reason to suspect that the high frequency of tokens of length 3 is due to an artifact in the post-processing chain.

Turning to the tail of the distribution, however, there are a few words longer than 40, and even longer than 1,000 characters. Taking a closer look at these (Figure 5.3 gives some examples), it becomes evident that some of them are regular German words or are due to colloquial writing style (e. g., phrasal pre-modification of nouns), but others clearly point to shortcomings in both non-linguistic and linguistic post processing. Yet, the percentage of words over 40 characters in length is less than 0.005% in this particular sample, including long regular German words alongside a number of non-words, so the problem seems to be rather negligible for most applications of the corpus.

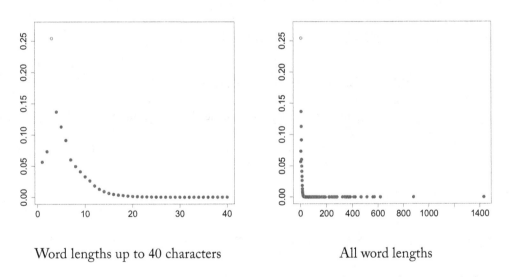

Word lengths up to 40 characters   All word lengths

Figure 5.1: Distribution of word lengths (measured in number of characters) in a sample ($n = 14.8$ million tokens) of the German DECOW2012 corpus.

Turning now to the distribution of sentence length in the sample, given in Figure 5.4, the general shape is of the expected positively skewed type. However, sentences of length 1 are heav-

Rank	Freq	Type	Rank	Freq	Type
1	348450	die	11	93237	ein
2	344946	und	12	87815	für
3	323051	der	13	73666	dem
4	159149	das	14	64336	des
5	147918	ich	15	59375	als
6	146950	ist	16	57841	...
7	140616	den	17	57808	man
8	121540	mit	18	56971	Die
9	112725	von	19	55475	sie
10	95628	auf	20	54600	bei

Figure 5.2: Words of length 3: first part of frequency list, generated from a sample of the German DECOW2012 corpus ($n = 14.8$ million tokens).

Length	"Word"	Class
60	Mein-Kind-hat-Nix-Gemacht-Lehrer-Sind-An-Allem-Schuld-Mütter	long noun modifier
60	e3.jpg&width=800m&height=600m&bodyTag=%3CBODY-%20style%3D%22m	partial URL
71	-HKEY_CURRENT_USER\Software\Microsoft\MediaPlayer-\Player\RecentFileList	part of a system path
79	SachverständigengutachtenSachverständigerSäuglingserstaus-stattungSchadensersatz	post-processing error (deleted whitespace)
100	er-Dachtr%C3%A4gersystem%2FZ%C3%B6lzer-Dachtr%C3-%A4ger+Zubeh%C3%B6r%2FSeitlicher+Hublift&seite=shop/	partial URL
266	< Ich habe es das erste mal gemalt und bin froh, dass es überhaupt was geworden ist. Sowohl bei Renamon als auch bei Wargreymon hatte ich die ganze Zeit Vorlagen daneben liegen. Bei WGmon hatte ich auch Glück, eine Vorlage zu finden, wo es eine Ähnliche Pose hatte >	tokenization error (sequence between angle brackets treated as XML-tag)

Figure 5.3: Tokens over 40 characters in length (from a sample of DECOW2012).

ily over-represented, which calls for further assessment. Figure 5.5 shows a number of different sentences of length 1 from the sample, sorted by frequency. Several cases can be distinguished here:

1. Artifacts of post-processing: For this particular corpus, URLs and emails addresses in the documents were replaced with the strings *urlblank* and *emailblank*, respectively. In a considerable number of cases, these ended up as (pseudo-)sentences, partly because the annotation scheme for this corpus does not allow material to be outside of a sentence region. Any ma-

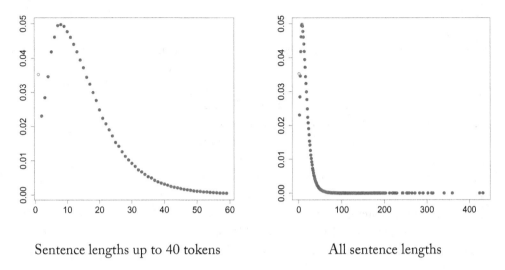

Sentence lengths up to 40 tokens   All sentence lengths

Figure 5.4: Distribution of sentence lengths (measured in number of tokens) in a sample ($n = 14.8$ million tokens, 1 million sentences) of the German DECOW2012 corpus.

terial occurring in between two recognized sentences was thus labeled as a sentence as well. A similar explanation holds for *NEUMARKT*, the name of a town which precedes every individual text on the page of a local newspaper (shown in Figure 5.6). Ideally, such items would be recognized and labeled as headings or sub-headings, not sentences.

2. Incorrect tokenization: Broken phpBB emoticons (e. g., *:mrgreen*, *:rolleyes*) and the broken abbreviation *Evtl* (for *Eventuell*, 'perhaps'), which the tokenizer did not recognize as such, probably as an effect of capitalization.

3. Failure in boilerplate removal: *mehr*/*Mehr* ('more') certainly derives from the 'read more...' links in the original HTML documents, which ideally should have been recognized and removed during post-processing. Figure 5.6 illustrates this. Similarly, *top* is a navigational element that should not show up in the final corpus, and *object* probably comes from programming code snippets.

4. Regular one-word utterances: *Danke* ('thank you'), *Ja* ('yes'), *Nein* ('no'), *Warum* ('why')

5. Emoticons: Tokens such as :D : (:p may or may not be viewed as equivalents to sentences, depending on linguistic decisions. It is a question of corpus design that has to be answered individually.

As for the tail of the distribution, there are strikingly long sentences (consisting of 200 or more tokens). For reasons of space, we will not illustrate these with examples, but rather name a few cases that are likely to turn up:

1. Extremely long normal sentences: This is more likely to happen if the characters relevant for sentence boundary detection are restricted to [.?!] and do not include e. g., [;:].

2. Tokenization errors: If the tokenizer is configured to leave XML tags intact, then precautions must be taken for occurrences of angled brackets that are not part of an XML tag. Otherwise, several words (in the worst case, entire sentences) may end up as a single token in the corpus.

3. Non-normalized punctuation (see Section 4.4.1): If omitted whitespace after an end-of-sentence punctuation mark is not corrected for, and the tokenizer is not configured to handle such cases, the sentence boundary will not be detected, resulting in two or more sentences glued together.

4. Genre-specific style of writing: Some text types tolerate a relaxed use of punctuation marks. E. g., postings to discussion forums often contain hardly any periods at all, even if they comprise several sentences.

5. Lists and enumerations in the original HTML document: As text from such elements often lacks end of sentence markers, all items of the list are likely to be treated as forming a single sentence.

In sum, then, the distribution of word and sentence length in this example reveals several weak points in the post-processing chain. At this point, if these shortcomings are judged as severe, adjustments can be made to the respective post-processing tools, and one or more of them can be re-applied to the data. It should be kept in mind, though, that some of the flaws illustrated above arise from non-trivial problems, for example classifying strings as a heading (for example, *NEUMARKT*) when they lack proper markup in the original HTML document, or detecting sentences with missing end-of-sentence punctuation. It is almost certain that large web corpora can never reach a degree of cleanliness comparable to traditional corpora. More often than not, re-doing post-processing steps at this stage will involve balancing time and effort against the potential gain of having fixed certain anomalies, and it may often be the case that knowing the characteristics and limitations of large web corpora is sufficient to avoid unwarranted conclusions in doing linguistic work with these corpora.

5.2.2   DUPLICATION

Imperfect (near-)duplicate removal on the document level might still leave duplicate sentences or paragraphs in the final corpus. Massive duplication of larger n-grams can be indicative of shortcomings in (near-)duplicate detection and failure in boilerplate removal. A first step in detecting such anomalies is searching for massively duplicated sentences. Figure 5.7 illustrates this with the counts for some repeated sentences in a sample (1 million sentences) of the German DE-COW2012 corpus. Among the repeated sentences, there are a number of short utterances like *Danke* ('Thank you') that could plausibly have been generated by different writers on different occasions, and this type of duplication is expected for very short sentences. They are marked 'R' in the table. On the other hand, the sentences marked 'B' are clearly cases of boilerplate that should

Freq.	Type	Freq.	Type
4554	urlblank	175	Nein
1367	:D	168	NEUMARKT
561	mehr	155	Ja
316	:rolleyes	146	Warum
272	:confused	146	top
242	^	139	:p
237	:(	137	:eek
220	emailblank	130	:cool
203	:-	113	Evtl
200	:lol	110	:mad
195	Danke	108	:mrgreen
189	Mehr	99	object
188	:wink	85	S.

Figure 5.5: Sentences of length 1: upper part of the frequency list for a sample of 1 million sentences from DECOW2012.

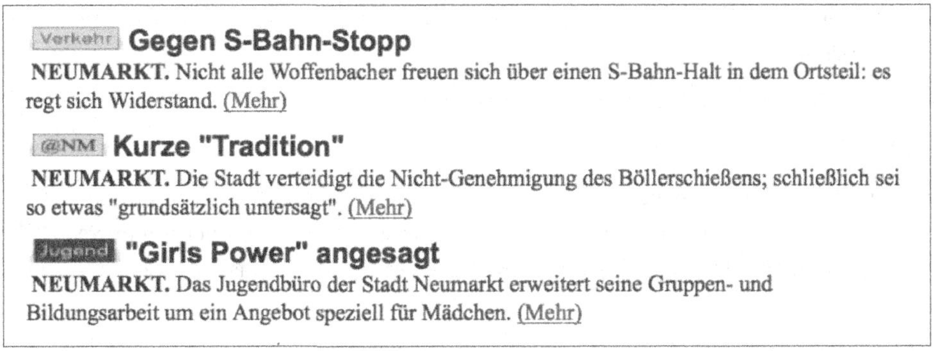

Figure 5.6: Where duplicated 1-token sentences (*NEUMARKT*; *Mehr*) originate: screenshot from a local German news website, `http://www.neumarktonline.de`.

have been removed in post processing, most of them originating from forum and blog software. One case in this sample (marked 'T') is the title of a show for which several online shops were selling tickets at the time of the crawl. It is thus not a prototypical instance of boilerplate, but it is not a prototypical instance of human-generated text either, which illustrates again the fact that distinguishing between 'good text' and 'bad text' is a delicate matter even conceptually. In any event, the clear cases of boilerplate that are detectable by looking at duplicated sentences may provide useful information when it comes to fine-tuning the post-processing tool chain. Since duplicated material does not necessarily surface in the form of sentences, it may also be worthwhile to inspect duplication of (reasonably large) n-grams.

Freq.	Sentence	Category
195	Danke	R
189	Mehr	B
175	Nein	R
160	Powered by vBulletin® Version 4.1.7 Copyright © 2011 Adduco Digital e.K. und vBulletin Solutions Inc. Alle Rechte vorbehalten	B
155	Ja	R
146	Warum	R
127	Um die detaillierte Vollansicht mit Formatierung und Bildern zu betrachten bitte hier klicken	B
94	Dieses ist eine vereinfachte Darstellung unseres Foreninhaltes	B
94	Der Preis ist einmalig und muss bei Verlängerung des Marktes nicht nochmals beglichen werden	B
83	Hallo	R
75	Quelle urlblank	B
64	Vielen Dank	R
62	Zünd an es kommt der Weihnachtsmann	T
59	Alle Rechte vorbehalten	B
58	Mit freundlichen Grüßen	R
58	Du kannst auf Beiträge in diesem Forum nicht antworten	B
54	Du kannst deine Beiträge in diesem Forum nicht löschen	B
53	Richtig	R
52	Schade	R
52	Es ist Ihnen nicht erlaubt Anhänge hochzuladen	B
51	Stimmt	R
50	Du darfst deine Beiträge in diesem Forum nicht ändern	B

Figure 5.7: Duplicated sentences in a sample of 1 million sentences of the German DECOW2012 web corpus. The 'B' cases are instances of boilerplate that were not properly removed; 'R' cases are regular, short German utterances; the status of the 'T' case is unclear (it is the title of a show announced on many ticket-selling websites).

5.3   MEASURING CORPUS SIMILARITY

One aspect of corpus evaluation is certainly the question of how the web corpus compares to other corpora. For example, a web corpus can be compared to other web corpora that went through a similar (or different) post-processing chain. Another interesting question to ask is how the web corpus compares with traditional, widely used corpora that have known characteristics. For example, is the web corpus larger, but otherwise similar to traditional corpora, or does it have its own properties that distinguish it from such corpora? Of course, at this point, the question arises of what it means for two corpora to be similar to each other, and there is not a simple single answer to this question.

For instance, similarity can be assessed in terms of corpus composition (text types, topics, authorship, etc.), an issue that will be briefly addressed in Section 5.6. Another way of examining the similarity of two corpora consists in computing some overall similarity measure by comparing the distribution of linguistic entities contained in the corpora, for example, the distribution of lexical items. The comparison may also be based on higher-level linguistic constructs (such as part-of-speech categories). In this case, however, the result will depend not only on properties of the corpora, but also on the accuracy of the linguistic processing tool(s), which may perform with different accuracy on different corpora and may thus introduce biases. A similar point is also made in Kilgarriff [2001], which we recommend as an entry point to corpus comparison in terms of similarity measures, and much of what follows in this section draws on it. Yet another method of comparing corpora is extracting keywords, either from individual documents or from the entire collection, and then use these in describing the corpora from a content-related point of view.

5.3.1 INSPECTING FREQUENCY LISTS

A simplistic approach to comparing corpora is to inspect frequency lists derived from them. For example, the table in Figure 5.8 lists the 20 most frequent common nouns in the French FR-COW2011 corpus and in the WaCKy initiative's frWaC corpus. The overlap seems to be substantial, even though the data for the two corpora were crawled several years apart and using different seed URL sets (thousands of seed URLs in the case of frWaC, and only ten in the case of FRCOW2011). Still, this kind of comparison is of course impressionistic and does not provide any real measure of the difference, nor does it answer the question of whether the two corpora are significantly similar to (or different from) each other. Next, we will therefore address corpus comparison from a hypothesis-testing perspective.

Rank	FRCOW 2011 (few seed URLs)	FRWAC (many seed URLs)
1	**année** 'year'	**site**
2	**travail** 'work'	**an**
3	**temps** 'time'	**travail**
4	**an** 'year'	**jour**
5	**jour** 'day'	**année**
6	pays 'country'	**service**
7	monde 'world'	**temps**
8	**vie** 'life'	article
9	**personne** 'person'	**personne**
10	homme 'man'	**projet**
11	**service**	information
12	**cas** 'case'	entreprise 'company'
13	**droit** 'right'	recherche '(re-)search'
14	effet 'effect'	**vie**
15	**projet** 'project'	**droit**
16	question	page
17	enfant 'child'	formation ('education')
18	**fois** 'time (occasion)'	commentaire 'comment'
19	place	**cas**
20	**site**	**fois**

Figure 5.8: The 20 most frequent common nouns in FRCOW2011 and frWaC.

5.3.2   HYPOTHESIS TESTING WITH χ^2

At first sight, it seems plausible that the χ^2 test for homogeneity could be used to test whether the two corpora are samples from the same population (or at least, from populations with the same distribution). In our context, the test compares the frequencies of a word type in the two corpora in the following way:

	Corpus 1	Corpus 2
word X	freq(X)	freq(X)
¬ **word X**	freq(¬X)	freq(¬X)

For the purpose of comparing two corpora with respect to the frequency of a word, the table has 2 columns and 2 rows, and the χ^2 statistic can be calculated using the formula in 5.1, where i and j are column and row numbers, respectively. O_{ij} is the observed value of a cell, and E_{ij} is the expected value of that cell given the marginal sums. The test statistic approximates a χ^2 distribution with one degree of freedom. If the expected value in a cell is less than 5, then Yate's continuity correction should be applied. However, given the high token counts in the upper part of a sorted frequency list, this will not be an issue in the following example, where the expected value of a cell E_{ij} is the corresponding row total multiplied by the corresponding column total, divided by the sum of all observations.

$$\chi^2 = \sum_{i,j=1}^{2} \frac{(O_{ij} - E_{ij})^2}{E_{ij}} \tag{5.1}$$

The null hypothesis is that a word has the same distribution in both corpora. If it cannot be rejected, then any difference in the frequency of a word would be assumed to be due to chance (sampling error), and there would be no reason to assume that the two corpora are samples from different populations. The alternative hypothesis states that there is a difference which chance alone is unlikely to have caused. If we assume the alternative hypothesis, we conclude that the word is distributed differently in the two corpora and that the two corpora are not random samples from the same population. Figure 5.9 illustrates this with data from two Spanish web corpora. A χ^2 statistic is calculated for each word (the example shows the 14 most frequent items, which happen to be the same in the two corpora). The p-values of the individual tests indicate that in five cases (*de, que, y, los, se*), the probability that the difference in frequency has arisen by chance alone is below 0.01.

In addition, a χ^2 test could be computed for the 14×2-table in 5.9 as a whole. In this example, the result would be $\chi^2 = 76.87$, p < .001 on 13 degrees of freedom, and this could be interpreted as showing that Corpus 1 and Corpus 2 differ substantially from one another.

Now, contrary to what these statistically significant differences suggest, Corpus 1 and Corpus 2 are in fact random samples from the same population (the same larger corpus ES-COW2012), thus the χ^2 test would seem to be too sensitive here. One reason is that the randomness assumption is generally violated when it comes to the distribution of words in texts

Word	Frequency		χ^2	p
	CORPUS 1	CORPUS 2		
de	6781719	6802262	32.99	<.001***
,	5627749	5633555	3.12	.077
la	3613946	3614049	0.001	.975
.	3574395	3579032	3.08	.079
que	2963992	2956662	9.36	<.010**
y	2642241	2653365	23.88	<.001***
en	2562028	2564809	1.53	.217
el	2450353	2446328	3.40	.065
a	1885112	1882813	1.44	.230
los	1597103	1603537	13.09	<.001***
del	1173860	1172623	0.67	.415
se	1139311	1143202	6.68	<.010**
las	1054729	1054924	0.02	.896
un	1001556	1000106	1.07	.302

Figure 5.9: χ^2 statistics calculated for the 14 most frequent word types in two Spanish web corpora (110 million tokens each).

(see e. g., Baayen, 2001). Their probability of occurrence has been shown to depend on variables such as genre, author, topic (cf. Church and Gale, 1995, for variation across texts) as well as on discourse-level cohesion (cf. Baayen, 2001, for variation within texts), in addition to structural constraints imposed by the grammar. As Kilgarriff [2001] points out, such differences in word frequency distributions do not generally average out, even when thousands of texts are joined to form a corpus.

The second reason hypothesis testing with χ^2 tests is not ideally suited for corpus comparison is that, other things being equal, the χ^2 statistic grows as a function of sample size. With huge sample sizes, even minor differences in the distribution of a word will provide enough evidence to reject the null hypothesis (see discussion in Kilgarriff, 2001). This second point can be illustrated by doubling the size of the two corpora, as shown in Figure 5.10. Again, Corpus 3 and Corpus 4 are random samples from the same population, but this time, the difference in frequency is significant for 9 out of 14 words.

5.3.3 HYPOTHESIS TESTING WITH SPEARMAN'S RANK CORRELATION

Another way to assess the similarity of two corpora which perhaps suggests itself is computing a Spearman correlation for (a number of lexical items from) ranked frequency lists of the two corpora. The null hypothesis in this case is that there is no (or only chance) correlation between the ranked frequency lists of Corpus 1 and Corpus 2. The alternative hypothesis states that the frequency ranks of Corpus 1 and Corpus 2 are correlated, and this can be interpreted as evidence that Corpus 1 and Corpus 2 bear a statistically significant similarity to each other. If there are no (or only a few) ties in the ranks, Spearman's correlation coefficient can be computed using the

Form	Corpus 3	Corpus 4	χ^2	p
de	13579307	13563617	9.65	<.010**
,	11264561	11274225	4.38	.036*
la	7227386	7236002	5.31	.021*
.	7157262	7150075	3.72	.054
que	5924861	5932089	4.53	.033*
y	5303604	5292011	12.98	<.001***
en	5117964	5123526	3.10	.078
el	4885947	4900224	21.31	<.001***
a	3766747	3773854	6.82	<.010**
los	3203514	3193313	16.49	<.001***
del	2340110	2338707	0.42	.515
se	2277149	2284887	13.27	<.001***
las	2105694	2109117	2.81	.094
un	1998736	2002337	3.27	.070

Figure 5.10: Doubling corpus size: χ^2 statistics calculated for the 14 most frequent word types in two Spanish web corpora (220 million tokens each).

simplified formula given in 5.2, where D is the difference in rank for a given item in Corpus 1 and Corpus 2, and n is the number of ranked pairs considered.

$$r_s = 1 - \frac{6 \sum D^2}{n(n^2 - 1)} \tag{5.2}$$

Figure 5.11 shows the result of calculating a Spearman correlation for the same two corpora that were used to illustrate the χ^2 test above. Since the frequency ranks for all 14 words considered here are the same in both corpora, the result is a perfect correlation ($r_s = 1$, $p < .001$), defeating the null hypothesis. The conclusion would be that Corpus 1 and Corpus 2 bear a statistically significant similarity to each other. Note that this seems rather incompatible with the conclusion that we would have to draw had we used the χ^2 test on the same data. It is interesting to see how the Spearman correlation behaves in case two rather dissimilar corpora are compared. Figure 5.12 shows the calculation for a comparison of Corpus 1 with a hypothetical Corpus X that has quite different frequencies and ranks for many of the words. But even in this case, the rank correlation is statistically significant ($p < 0.05$), indicating that the two corpora are similar. Thus, when used for hypothesis testing as in this example, the Spearman correlation is not a suitable measure because it tends to reject the null hypothesis even if there are linguistically interesting differences between two corpora. Moreover, as Kilgarriff [2001] notes, differences among the top-ranked items have the same impact on the correlation coefficient as differences between lower-ranked items, but from a linguistic perspective, differences among the first few ranks are arguably quite substantial, while differences among lower ranks are probably not.

Form	Corpus 1	Corpus 2	Rank Corpus 1	Rank Corpus 2	D	D^2
de	6781719	6802262	1	1	0	0
,	5627749	5633555	2	2	0	0
la	3613946	3614049	3	3	0	0
.	3574395	3579032	4	4	0	0
que	2963992	2956662	5	5	0	0
y	2642241	2653365	6	6	0	0
en	2562028	2564809	7	7	0	0
el	2450353	2446328	8	8	0	0
a	1885112	1882813	9	9	0	0
los	1597103	1603537	10	10	0	0
del	1173860	1172623	11	11	0	0
se	1139311	1143202	12	12	0	0
las	1054729	1054924	13	13	0	0
un	1001556	1000106	14	14	0	0

$$r_s = 1 - \frac{6 \sum D^2}{n(n^2 - 1)} = 1 - \frac{6 \times 0}{14(14^2 - 1)} = 1 - 0 = 1$$

Figure 5.11: Spearman's rank correlation calculated for the 14 most frequent lexical items in Corpus 1 and Corpus 2: a perfect correlation.

5.3.4   USING TEST STATISTICS WITHOUT HYPOTHESIS TESTING

As the above examples illustrate, if the question of whether two corpora are similar or different is answered by hypothesis testing, both χ^2 and the rank correlation fail to capture linguistic intuitions about what it means for two corpora to be similar or different. However, as opposed to testing a null hypothesis, such test statistics can also be used for ranking a set of candidates. For example, in detecting collocations, the t-statistic and other measures have been interpreted as indicators of collocation strength, without doing any hypothesis testing [Manning and Schütze, 1999, Ch. 5]. Similarly, Kilgarriff [2001] suggests to do away with hypothesis testing in comparing corpora, and instead use test statistics as a measure of relative similarity between corpora, without looking at p-values. While this approach does not provide a measure of similarity in absolute terms ("Corpus 1 and Corpus 2 have a statistically significant similarity"), it can be used to assess the relative similarity between corpora ("Corpus 1 is more similar to Corpus 2 than to Corpus 3"). The question of course remains as to which test statistic best captures a relevant notion of "similarity." Kilgarriff [2001] approaches this issue experimentally by preparing a set of different corpora, each of which has a different composition in terms of text types. A number of gold standard judgments about their similarity can thus be derived, and different test statistics can be evaluated as to how accurately they reflect these gold standard judgments. The main finding is that the χ^2 statistic outperforms both the Spearman correlation coefficient and several variants of cross-entropy measures. The procedure is to compute a χ^2 statistic for a $2 \times m$ contingency table for m most frequent words of Corpus 1 and Corpus 2 taken together (Kilgarriff, 2001, re-

Form	Corpus 1	Corpus X	Rank 1	Rank X	D	D^2
de	6781719	2446328	1	8	-7	49
,	5627749	2564809	2	7	-5	25
la	3613946	2653365	3	6	-3	9
.	3574395	2956662	4	5	-1	1
que	2963992	3579032	5	4	1	1
y	2642241	3614049	6	3	3	9
en	2562028	5633555	7	2	5	25
el	2450353	6802262	8	1	7	49
a	1885112	1882813	9	9	0	0
los	1597103	1000106	10	14	4	16
del	1173860	1054924	11	13	2	4
se	1139311	1143202	12	12	0	0
las	1054729	1172623	13	11	2	4
un	1001556	1603537	14	10	4	16
						$\sum = 208$

$$r_s = 1 - \frac{6 \sum D^2}{n(n^2 - 1)} = 1 - \frac{6 \times 208}{14(14^2 - 1)} = 1 - \frac{1248}{2730} = \mathbf{0.543}, p < .05$$

Figure 5.12: Spearman rank correlation between two rather dissimilar corpora: still a significant correlation coefficient.

ports that $m = 500$ works reasonably well). The χ^2 value is normalized by the degrees of freedom $(m - 1)$ and can then be used for pairwise comparisons of corpora (which must be of the same size, though, because the χ^2 value increases with absolute frequency).

5.4   COMPARING KEYWORDS

Another option for assessing the similarity of corpora is to compare lists of keywords extracted from them. As opposed to the inspection of frequency lists as shown in Figure 5.8 above, keywords are not just words that are frequent in a corpus (or document), but words that are in some sense characteristic of a corpus (or document). A word's degree of *key-ness* in a corpus (or document) can be established in a variety of ways, but it often involves frequency. Crucially, key-ness in this sense is a relative notion: a word is characteristic of a text/document because there are other relevant documents/corpora of which the word is not (or less) characteristic. The reference point can be some other corpus of about the same size, or it can be a much larger (and usually more varied) corpus. Common approaches to keyword extraction compute a statistic from the frequency of each word occurring in a document (or corpus) and the frequency of the same word in the reference corpus. The statistic is then used to determine to what extent a word is characteristic of a document (or corpus). In addition, some approaches calculate a p-value for each statistic, and sometimes a measure of each word's dispersion (whether it is common to many documents or occurs in just a few) is taken into account as well. Approaches differ as to the statistic they use, for example:

- Ratio of relative frequencies (e. g., Damerau, 1993; Edmundson and Wyllys, 1961; Kilgar-riff, 2012),
- Yule's [1944] difference coefficient (e. g., Hofland and Johansson, 1982),
- χ^2 (e. g., Scott, 1997),
- -2 Log-Likelihood (e. g., Scott, 2001),
- Mann-Whitney U (Kilgarriff, 2001),
- term frequency by inverse document frequency (tf-idf, going back to Spärck Jones, 1972).

The different statistics used for keyword extraction may result in quite different keyword lists for the same pair of corpora. We will illustrate this by comparing keywords extracted on the basis of χ^2 with keywords obtained using the ratio of relative frequencies.

5.4.1   KEYWORD EXTRACTION WITH χ^2

A χ^2 value is computed from a 2×2 table for each word type in the joined corpus (Corpus 1 + Corpus 2). That value is multiplied by the sign of the first table cell's Observed-Expected value, which is positive if a word is over-represented in Corpus 1 and negative in case it is under-represented. Without this step, it is impossible to tell whether a given word is characteristic of Corpus 1 or Corpus 2. The word list is then sorted on the resulting score. The words on top of the sorted list are over-represented in Corpus 1 (with respect to Corpus 2) and are thus considered to be keywords of Corpus 1. Figures 5.13 and 5.14 illustrate this with two samples from the German DECOW2012 corpus.

The number of function words on these two lists is particularly striking. If the aim of keyword extraction is to draw conclusions about prominently represented domains in the corpora, then function words are rather poor keywords. However, function words ending up as keywords may warrant conclusions about text types/genres that are characteristic of a corpus. In the present example, the fact that first and second person pronouns, emoticons, and non-standard spellings (*hab* < *habe* '(I) have') are among the most characteristic words of Corpus 2 suggests that this corpus contains rather informal text types (like postings to discussion forums). We will get back to the issue of content words below when we contrast the results to the list of keywords obtained using the ratio of relative frequencies.

5.4.2   KEYWORD EXTRACTION USING THE RATIO OF RELATIVE FREQUENCIES

The ratio of relative frequencies was suggested as a measure early in research on automatic document summarization and indexing [Edmundson and Wyllys, 1961], and it has also been used for extracting multi-word keywords [Damerau, 1993]. The technique consists in dividing a word's relative frequency in a document by its relative frequency in a reference document collection, which can be general (mixed domains) or domain specific. Kilgarriff [2012] shows how keywords from different frequency bands can be obtained by varying the value of a smoothing constant

Score	Word	Translation	f Corpus 1	f Corpus 2
213857	Selbstbewusstsein	'self-consciousness'	230086	7103
180761	der	'the'	25823958	23332624
112942	Stärken	'strengths'	147041	13782
110867	des	'of.the'	5467541	4511218
109470	stärken	'strengthen'	150609	16807
81735	in	'in'	14531108	13291861
80314	Niederösterreich	'Lower Austria	81732	997
69230	und	'and'	27615823	26209999
67723	Steiermark	'Styria'	69845	1165
61955	Schwächen	'weaknesses'	101680	17034
58046	Sie	'you'	2389178	1929354
48998	Selbstbewusstseinstraining	'self-consciousness training'	48100	3
45075	Die	'the'	4725965	4176917
41216	Oberösterreich	'Upper Austria'	43930	1217
38921	werden	'become'	3889092	3424772
33635	,	,	61275629	60440998
33447	die	'the'	26896810	26075513
33069	wir	'we'	2751969	2388203
32967	Gott	'God'	277819	161587
27182	»	»	499957	355500
26135	durch	'through'	2028104	1749480
25822	uns	'us'	1432263	1196461
25367	von	'from'	8958078	8458655
24745	Beispiele	'examples'	95118	38807
24657	«	«	437106	308515
23838	Menschen	'people'	804843	633205
23655	zur	'to.the'	1887285	1631892
23466	In	'in	1267897	1056218
23359	sich	'oneself'	7073007	6636924
23056	Coaching	'coaching'	32678	3958

Figure 5.13: Corpus-wise keyword extraction with χ^2: top 30 words over-represented in Corpus 1. Score $= \chi^2 \times sgn(O_{1,1} - E_{1,1})$

(smoothing is necessary anyway to avoid division by zero in case the frequency of a word in the reference corpus is zero). For every word occurring in at least one of the two corpora, the relative frequency in each corpus is calculated after adding a smoothing constant to both numerator and denominator. Next, the ratio of the relative frequencies in Corpus 1 and Corpus 2 is taken, and the list of all ratios is sorted. The words at the top and bottom of the list are the keywords of Corpus 1 and Corpus 2, respectively. Figures 5.15 and 5.16 show the list of keywords generated by this method for the same two samples which were used in the χ^2 example above.

As opposed to the keywords extracted with χ^2, there are no function words at all here. The keywords of Corpus 1 are dominated by content words from the domain of psychological coaching, most of which do not occur at all in Corpus 2. On further inspection, this turns out to be a combined failure of the crawling strategy that was used to build the corpus (breadth-first with additional Heritrix host bias, see Section 2.3), and the technique used for near duplicate detection. Corpus 1 contains several thousand documents from the server of a life coaching company. The documents are virtually identical, except that a different name of a town is inserted in

Score	Word	Translation	f Corpus 1	f Corpus 2
-49228	es	'it'	7191558	8203365
-52339	!	!	3539669	4250013
-55500	jetzt	'now'	1093904	1497137
-58057	so	'so'	4078118	4881829
-58090	meine	'my'	743321	1086311
-61785	was	'what'	2368986	2994141
-62641	wenn	'if'	2525537	3175758
-62847	:zustimm:	'agree	4	64046
-65120	bin	'am'	898077	1296452
-68224	das	'the'	11114277	12601969
-68699	:	:	7361865	8552945
-69360	Du	'you'	856126	1258723
-70448	dann	'then'	2705021	3418243
-73501	:-D	:-D	4080	86533
-74531	schon	'already'	2299966	2975671
-79816	mich	'me'	1776035	2391232
-80099	auch	'too'	7618001	8919734
-99309	da	'there'	2125894	2876793
-102364	aber	'but'	3900764	4932552
-115949	du	'you'	1501636	2189889
-117379	hab	'have'	606783	1065271
-138531	nicht	'not'	9679787	11587724
-144946	habe	'have'	1725867	2552673
-166247	ja	'yes'	1806276	2714682
-176159	mir	'me'	2190317	3215638
-176735	Ich	'I'	2664716	3791898
-186177	?	?	3889053	5278796
-186838	mal	'once'	2000220	3014011
-333374	...	...	3418151	5189644
-709423	ich	'I'	8606043	12673625

Figure 5.14: Corpus-wise keyword extraction with χ^2: top 30 words over-represented in Corpus 2. Score= $\chi^2 \times sgn(O_{1,1} - E_{1,1})$

almost each sentence. This makes the sets of n-grams derived from the documents quite different, leading to the failure of the shingling approach as described in Section 3.5.3. The keywords as they appear here are those occurring frequently in all those documents. Thus, as a side effect, the keyword list sheds some light on the limitations of this approach to near duplicate removal.

As for the lower part of the keyword list (Figure 5.16), our assumption that Corpus 2 contains more text written in an informal style than Corpus 1 seems to be confirmed here. But, interestingly, the majority among the top 30 keywords are emoticons (in the phpBB style) here, while χ^2 returned predominantly function words. The reason for this difference is that the ratio of relative frequencies does not depend on the words' absolute frequencies, whereas the χ^2 grows with increasing absolute frequency of the words even if the ratio remains constant, as illustrated in Figure 5.17. Since function words normally have very high frequencies, they can be expected to turn up as keywords if χ^2 is used as a measure.

Ratio	Word	Translation	f Corpus 1	f Corpus 2
14193	IntSel®-Selbstbewusstseinstraining	'IntSel® self-consciousness training'	13929	0
12252	Selbstbewusstseinstraining	'self-consciousness training'	48100	3
11414	IntSel®-Selbstbewusstseinstrainings	'IntSel® self-consciousness trainings'	11201	0
7253	moviac	moviac (NE)	7118	0
5022	Kinder-Selbstbewusstseins-Coach	'children's self-consciousness coach'	4928	0
3876	www.theaterstuebchen.de	www.theaterstuebchen.de	3803	0
2876	Selbstbewusstseinstrainer	'self-consciousness coach'	2822	0
2854	'schmökern	'to browse'	2800	0
2853	IntSel®-Wertekonzept	'IntSel® scheme of values'	2799	0
2853	IntSel®-Stärkenleiter	'IntSel® scale of strengths'	2799	0
2853	Angst-Vermeidungsstrategien	'fear avoidance strategies'	2799	0
2853	'Austherapierte	'healed persons'	2799	0
2693	HR-Lieblingsschiff	'HR favorite ship'	2642	0
2613	Schwehm	Schwehm (NE)	17949	6
2158	www.bauemotion.de	www.bauemotion.de	2117	0
2068	:futsch:	emoticon	2029	0
1961	Litaraturmarkt	'literature market'	1924	0
1721	Thor'al	Thor'al (NE)	1688	0
1631	Grujicic	Grujicic (NE)	1600	0
1591	:fletch:	emoticon	1561	0
1554	Terror-Die	terror-the	1524	0
1550	Architektur-Meldungen	'architecture news'	1520	0
1496	Beamt-er/	'state employee'	1467	0
1469	91785	91785	2883	1
1464	Systemcoach	'system coach'	2872	1
1438	Party-Highlight	'party highlight'	1410	0
1435	Tiergefahren	'danger from animals'	1407	0
1434	Tybrang	Tybrang (NE)	1406	0
1433	Titelvertei-digung	'title defense'	1405	0
1433	Riesen-Herausforderer	'big contender'	1405	0

Figure 5.15: Corpus-wise keyword extraction using the ratio of relative frequencies: top 30 words over-represented in Corpus 1.

5.4.3   VARIANTS AND REFINEMENTS

While the above examples illustrate the basic mechanism, there are several refinements of the methods which address various shortcomings of the basic approach. To begin with, using word forms has the disadvantage that homonyms (such as *bank*, *house*, *handle*, each of which has several meanings) are counted together. On the other hand, inflected forms of the same lemma are counted separately (such as *give*, *gives*, *gave*, *given*). This is undesirable in most contexts, since keywords are usually meant to represent central concepts of a text, not formal aspects. This problem does not arise if words are disambiguated (morphologically, syntactically, semantically) before measuring their frequencies. Such an approach would thus operate with lemmas, or pairs of the form ⟨word form, POS⟩ or ⟨word form, sense⟩.

Alternatively, keyword extraction can be based on the dispersion of a word in the two corpora, for instance, measured in terms of a word's document frequency (the number of documents it occurs in; see Scott, 2001, for an example). It is also possible to combine a word's frequency

Ratio	Word	Translation	f Corpus 1	f Corpus 2
4.268E-04	:five:	emoticon	1	4774
4.265E-04	@vandeStonehill	@vandeStonehill	0	2388
4.265E-04	#WeLove	#WeLove	0	2388
4.265E-04	#HighSchoolMusical3	#HighSchoolMusical3	0	2388
4.208E-04	:aargh:	emoticon	0	2420
4.195E-04	:meinemeinung	emoticon	0	2428
4.189E-04	|supergri	emoticon	0	2431
4.125E-04	:zickig:	emoticon	0	2469
4.107E-04	*seh	*seh	0	2480
4.098E-04	|kopfkrat	emoticon	0	2485
4.096E-04	kostenlose-urteile.de	kostenlose-urteile.de	0	2486
4.072E-04	Migrantenrat	'immigrants' board'	1	5003
4.072E-04	MV-Politiker	'MV-politician'	0	2501
3.971E-04	berlin.business-on.de	berlin.business-on.de	0	2565
3.731E-04	:fürcht:	emoticon	0	2730
3.655E-04	:leiderja:	emoticon	0	2787
3.473E-04	Bollywoodsbest	Bollywoodsbest	0	2933
3.329E-04	Fotoserver	'photo server'	0	3060
3.192E-04	:urgs:	emoticon	0	3191
3.174E-04	:habenmuss:	emoticon	0	3209
3.168E-04	Stachelhausen	Stachelhausen (NE)	1	6431
2.906E-04	:rothlol:	emoticon	0	3505
2.637E-04	Juusuf	Juusuf (NE)	0	3863
2.489E-04	:zumgluecknein:	emoticon	0	4092
2.136E-04	:zufrieden:	emoticon	0	4770
1.953E-04	:menno:	emoticon	0	5217
1.818E-04	@ProSieben	@ProSieben	0	5602
1.682E-04	:dollschaem:	emoticon	0	6056
1.331E-04	:traeum:	emoticon	0	7656
1.281E-04	:dollfreu:	emoticon	0	7955

Figure 5.16: Corpus-wise keyword extraction using the ratio of relative frequencies: top 30 words over-represented in Corpus 2.

Corpus 1		Corpus 2			
f absolute	f relative	f absolute	f relative	Ratio of rel. freqs.	χ^2
50	.05	100	.1	0.5	17.3
100	.1	200	.2	0.5	38.4
200	.2	400	.4	0.5	94.3

Figure 5.17: χ^2 vs. ratio of relative frequencies in keyword extraction, illustrated by two corpora of 1,000 tokens each.

and a measure of its dispersion for computing its key-ness (e. g., Rayson, 2003; for an overview of different measures of dispersion, see Gries, 2008).

Moreover, keywords can be extracted not only for a corpus as a whole, but also for individual documents. An example is Scott's [1997] approach, which compares the frequency list of each document in Corpus 1 with the frequency list of Corpus 2. Corpus 1 as a whole can then be characterized by computing *key-keywords* (words that are keywords in many documents).

Finally, a very prominent approach to document-wise keyword extraction that combines frequency and dispersion of a word is based on term frequency by inverse document frequency. TF-IDF was originally suggested in Spärck Jones [1972] for term weighting in the context of document retrieval, and it is widely used today in many variants (see Manning et al., 2009, Ch. 6 for an overview). The underlying assumption is that a term is more characteristic of a document if it occurs frequently in that document, but does not occur in many other documents. In its most basic form, tf-idf is calculated as shown in 5.3, where $TF_{t,d}$ is the frequency of term t in document d, N is the total number of documents in the corpus that serves as reference point, and DF_t is the number of documents in that corpus which contain term t at least once.

$$TF.IDF_{t,d} = TF_{t,d} \cdot \log \frac{N}{DF_t} \tag{5.3}$$

Summing up the main points of this section, we have seen that assessing corpus similarity in terms of hypothesis testing leads to uninformative results from a linguistic point of view. On the other hand, the test statistics themselves can be used as a measure of relative similarity between corpora. From among the many variants of keyword extraction, we illustrated two methods whose results converged only partially, indicating that it is probably useful to apply more than one such method and compare the results.

5.5   EXTRINSIC EVALUATION

Extrinsic evaluation of a corpus means judging it in the context of a particular task and often involves a comparison with other corpora. As Kilgarriff et al. [in prep.] point out, a broad range of applications require similar properties of a corpus (e. g., low rate of duplication, high degree of cleanliness) and target "language in general" (e. g., dictionaries and many NLP tools). Thus, evaluating a corpus with respect to one not too specialized task arguably also sheds light on its quality with respect to more or less related tasks, and perhaps also indicates its general usefulness for typical linguistic applications. Extrinsic evaluation of web corpora has been performed in a variety of areas, ranging from classical linguistic applications (e. g., compiling lists of synonyms and collocations) to the training of NLP tools (e. g., spell checkers, POS taggers).

For example, in the domain of NLP applications, Liu and Curran [2006] find that using their 10 billion token web corpus of English as a training set for (a particular sub-task of) automatic spelling correction produces results similar to when the system is trained on the English Gigaword corpus (2 billion tokens of newspaper text; Graff and Cieri, 2003). In addition, training the system on their web corpus yields better results than training on search engine counts, which again underlines the advantages of using static, full-text corpora. Giesbrecht and Evert's [2009] comparison of different part-of-speech taggers, though not originally conceived as an evaluation of the corpora involved, nevertheless affords some conclusions as to the suitability of using a web corpus as training data for a (particular) POS tagger.

Distributional semantics, and in particular the automatic construction of thesauri (extended synonym lists for a given target word), is another area that has figured prominently in the extrinsic evaluation of corpora. In general terms, the procedure is to establish a gold standard of (quasi-) synonyms for a set of target words and then compare it with a set of synonyms automatically extracted from each of the candidate corpora. Individual studies differ in the details of how the gold standard is constructed and in the technical details concerning the identification of synonyms (type of context used in constructing the vectors, calculation of similarity between vectors). Frequently, the results of such studies suggest that traditional corpora yield better results than web corpora of about the same size, but are outperformed by larger web corpora. For example, building on work by Curran and Moens [2002], Liu and Curran [2006] find that their 10 billion tokens web corpus of English performs equally well at the thesaurus task as the 2 billion tokens English Gigaword corpus, but that a sample of 2 billion tokens from their web corpus does not. A similar result is reported in Versley and Panchenko [2012], who compare a number of web corpora (two purpose-made German web corpora and the German deWaC corpus) with a traditional corpus of newspaper text (TüPP-D/Z; Müller, 2004). Faruqui and Padó [2010] study the effect of augmenting a NER system (Named Entity Recognition) with distributional information about terms, thus incorporating semantic generalizations. Their main finding is that it makes very little or no difference in practice whether the similarity clustering is done using a 175M tokens German newswire corpus (Huge German Corpus) or a sample of the German deWaC of the same size.[3]

Another application suitable to the evaluation of corpora is the extraction of collocations. Similarly to the thesaurus task, this usually involves defining a gold standard set of collocations for a given set of target words. Collocations are automatically extracted from the candidate corpora and compared to the gold standard, and measures such as precision and recall can be computed to characterize the suitability of a given corpus for this particular task. For example, Ferraresi et al. [2008] find that their English and French web corpora (ukWaC and frWaC, respectively) are comparable to a balanced, traditional corpus (such as the BNC) in terms of suitability for a specific lexicographic purpose, namely a simulated revision of an English-French bilingual dictionary. Kilgarriff et al. [in prep.] evaluate a number of English and Czech corpora, both web-derived and traditional, on the collocation extraction task. Apart from discussing the role of gold standard construction, their main finding is that large corpus sizes tend to yield considerably better results, which means that web corpora (the ones used in the study are in the range of 10 billion tokens) are in an advantageous position with respect to smaller, traditional corpora. On the other hand, corpus annotation also plays a significant role, which is evidenced by the fact that collocation extraction from a (smaller) parsed corpus outperforms the much larger web corpus in the case of Czech. See also Biemann et al. [in prep.] for an evaluation of different web corpora and the BNC with respect to collocation extraction.

---

[3]http://www.ims.uni-stuttgart.de/forschung/ressourcen/korpora/hgc.html

To sum up, corpora can be evaluated with respect to a variety of tasks, some of which we briefly illustrated above. Many of these studies converge on the finding that web corpora do not generally perform noticeably worse than traditional corpora of the same size. Large web corpora frequently outperform smaller, traditional corpora, for instance when a specific task values the amount of available data more highly than the cleanliness of a corpus.

5.6   CORPUS COMPOSITION

When building a corpus based on a web crawl, documents are usually not sampled following a pre-established stratification scheme. In the best case, one might end up with a random sample of the (relevant part of the) WWW, but even in this case, the exact composition of the final corpus is not known and needs to be established after corpus construction. Documents in a collection can be classified along a large number of axes. A basic distinction in corpus composition can be drawn between external criteria (situational determinants such as topic, genre, mode of publication, etc.) and internal criteria (linguistic characteristics of a document; cf. Atkins et al., 1992; Biber, 1993). Among the external criteria, another distinction can be made between content-related dimensions (such as topic or domain) and other dimensions. Web documents are a challenge in this respect because some of them instantiate text types/genres that were not usually present in traditional (i. e., non-web) document collections. Recent years have seen a number of extensions of more traditional classification schemes to accommodate web genres (e. g., Biber and Kurjian, 2007; Rehm et al., 2008; Sinclair, 1996; *Open Directory Project* and many more), but there is no such thing as an established inventory of web genres. A variety of aspects of web genres is discussed in Mehler et al. [2010], which we recommend for approaching this topic. An example of a classification scheme is Sharoff [2006] (based on the EAGLES scheme), which posits five major dimensions: "authorship, mode (aka channel), knowledge expected from the audience, the aim of text production and the generalized domain."

5.6.1   ESTIMATING CORPUS COMPOSITION

Once a classification scheme is chosen, the classification itself can be carried out manually or automatically. By manually annotating a sample from the corpus, the distribution of a given variable in the population (which in this case is the corpus) can be estimated within a desired confidence interval. In order to train an automatic classifier, hand-annotated training data is usually needed as well, so manual annotation is probably the first step both for estimating corpus composition, and for automatic classification of the documents. We will not deal with the latter here (but see, for example, Sebastiani, 2002, for a survey of automated text categorization in the context of machine learning; Sharoff, 2010 for an application to web corpora). When hand-annotation is carried out in order to estimate the relative frequency of a category in the population, the size of the confidence interval must be balanced against the sample size. The point here is that hand-coding of a few hundred documents (as a minimum) is necessary in order to stay within acceptable confidence intervals (e. g., not greater than $\pm 5\%$) even in the worst case where a category makes up for 50%

of the data. When the annotation task is shared across several annotators, it is advisable to code a number of documents in parallel, check the inter-annotator agreement and, if necessary, clarify the application of the annotation guidelines before proceeding with the annotation.

5.6.2 MEASURING CORPUS COMPOSITION

Ciaramita and Baroni [2006] suggest a procedure for determining whether a corpus is "reasonably varied in terms of the topics (and, perhaps, textual types) it represents." The aim of these authors is not to collect a random sample of documents from the WWW, but rather to gather a collection of documents that is balanced in the sense that no topic or text type is heavily over-represented in it (i. e., a corpus which is deliberately biased with respect to a random sample, in a way considered favorable). Their procedure consists in calculating the distance of the target corpus to each one of a number of corpora that are deliberately biased toward some topic or text type. Biased corpora can be built by applying the BootCaT method (see 2.3.2, also for restrictions of the BootCaT method which apply as of today) on appropriately biased collections of word tuples. Distance is based on word frequencies and measured as relative entropy (or Kullback-Leibler distance, Kullback and Leibler, 1951). For each corpus, the distances to all other corpora are averaged to yield a mean distance. The expectation is that, if the target corpus is unbiased ("varied"), it arguably has a smaller mean distance than all biased corpora (because it is somewhere "in between" all these biased corpora). However, this method only makes sense if the corpus builders share Ciaramita and Baroni's [2006] ideal of a varied corpus. If, on the other hand, the goal in constructing a web corpus is something close to a uniform random sample of the accessible web, then the method does not apply.

5.6.3 INTERPRETING CORPUS COMPOSITION

Once the composition of a web corpus is known (or rather: has been estimated), it can be compared to the composition of other corpora. One question that has played a role in recent years is whether the composition of web corpora bears enough similarity to established, traditionally compiled corpora to be considered as alternatives in situations where more data is needed than traditional corpora can provide. Many of the corpora that are widely used in Corpus Linguistics aim at representativeness and are balanced, meaning that their composition reflects a ratio that the corpus designers establish in advance, according to what they think a balanced corpus should contain. The Brown corpus, the LOB corpus, the British National Corpus, and the German DWDS corpus are all balanced in this sense. Very large web corpora, on the other hand, are typically not balanced, because they are not obtained on the basis of a stratified sampling scheme, but by collecting documents more or less randomly from the web. If no measures are taken to correct for this, the composition of a web corpus is likely to be a result of the specific crawling strategy, plus potential biases introduced by post processing steps that discard certain documents for some reason or other.

Balance and the question of how representativeness can be achieved in corpus design can be considered from quite different perspectives (see, among many others, Atkins et al., 1992; Biber, 1993):

- Production: Corpus composition should reflect the distribution of texts produced in a speech community.
- Reception: Corpus composition should reflect the impact (number of recipients) of different text types (e. g., Leech, 2007).
- Relevance: Corpus composition should reflect the importance/influence of a text type, etc., in a speech community (discussed in Biber, 1993).

Determining any of these variables with any certainty is practically unfeasible, and for some of them, such as cultural relevance, it is not even clear how they could possibly be measured [Hunston, 2008, 162; McEnery et al., 2006, 16].

Another problem concerning balance is that

[…] arguments that a particular corpus is representative, or balanced, are inevitably circular, in that the categories we are invited to observe are artifacts of the design procedure [Hunston, 2008, 164]

From this perspective, the fact that typical web corpora are not balanced does not appear to be too serious a drawback, especially because their usually very large size has the potential to make up for it. As Leech [2007, 138] puts it:

[…] in general, the larger a corpus is, and the more diverse it is in terms of genres and other language varieties, the more balanced and representative it will be.

Of course, all that can be said about a corpus which is based on a random sample from a segment of the web is that it represents the distribution of different text types, topics, etc., within this segment of the web. Such a corpus might be considered highly valuable by some, and totally useless by others, which underlines the fact that there are no good or bad corpora in absolute terms. Rather, we totally agree with Hunston [2008] and others that a corpus can only be judged with respect to a particular purpose. It may also be useful to think of corpus construction as a cyclic process, in which

th[e] corpus is used and analyzed and its strengths and weaknesses identified and reported. In the light of this experience and feedback the corpus is enhanced by the addition or deletion of material and the cycle is repeated continually. [Atkins et al., 1992, 4]

We close this chapter with a quote from [McEnery et al., 2006, 73]:

Corpus-building is of necessity a marriage of perfection and pragmatism. […] It is advisable to base your claims on your corpus and avoid unreasonable generalizations.

5.7 SUMMARY

In this chapter, we have exemplified some ways of assessing a corpus's properties and quality, mostly under the premise that corpus quality is at best a relative notion. Some simple but effective techniques which work corpus-internally (e. g., examining word and sentence length distributions) were demonstrated. Other methods which we have introduced work by comparing aspects of the corpus, like word frequencies or keywords, to other corpora. These can be used, for example, to compare a web corpus to some reference corpus, or specialized (biased) corpora to more general corpora. All these techniques have the added advantage of potentially revealing flaws in the crawling and post-processing procedures as introduced in Chapters 2–4. In addition, we introduced the notion of extrinsic, task-oriented corpus evaluation and presented examples from the areas of automatic thesaurus building and collocation extraction. Finally, we briefly discussed how information about the composition of a corpus, which is often available for traditionally compiled corpora as an artifact of the stratified sampling procedure, has to be collected after corpus construction when it comes to web corpora. The results of such an assessment of corpus composition can also be used to compare the web corpus to other corpora.

Bibliography

Abiteboul, S., Preda, M., and Cobena, G. (2003). Adaptive on-line page importance computation. In *Proceedings of the 12th International Conference on World Wide Web*, WWW '03, pages 280–290, New York, NY, USA. ACM. DOI: 10.1145/775152.775192. 30

Abramson, M. and Aha, D. (2009). What's in a URL? Genre classification from URLs. Technical report, AAAI Technical Report WS-12-09. 35

Achlioptas, D., Clauset, A., Kempe, D., and Moore, C. (2005). On the bias of traceroute sampling: or, power-law degree distributions in regular graphs. In *Proceedings of the thirty-seventh annual ACM symposium on Theory of computing*, STOC '05, pages 694–703, New York, NY, USA. ACM. DOI: 10.1145/1060590.1060693. 30

Ahmad, F. and Kondrak, G. (2005). Learning a spelling error model from search query logs. In *HLT/EMNLP*. The Association for Computational Linguistics. DOI: 10.3115/1220575.1220695. 79

Almpanidis, G., Kotropoulos, C., and Pitas, I. (2007). Combining text and link analysis for focused crawling-an application for vertical search engines. *Inf. Syst.*, 32(6):886–908. DOI: 10.1016/j.is.2006.09.004. 35

Ando, R. K. and Lee, L. (2003). Mostly-unsupervised statistical segmentation of Japanese Kanji sequences. *Natural Language Engineering*, 9(2):127–149.
DOI: 10.1017/S1351324902002954. 66

Atkins, S., Clear, J., and Ostler, N. (1992). Corpus design criteria. *Literary and Linguistic Computing*, 7(1):1–16. DOI: 10.1093/llc/7.1.1. 106, 108

Baayen, H. R., Piepenbrock, R., and Gulikers, L. (1995). The CELEX lexical database (CD-ROM). Technical report, Linguistic Data Consortium, University of Pennsylvania, Philadelphia. 17

Baayen, R. H. (2001). *Word frequency distributions*. Kluwer, Dordrecht. DOI: 10.1007/978-94-010-0844-0. 95

Baeza-Yates, R., Castillo, C., and Efthimiadis, E. N. (2007). Characterization of national Web domains. *ACM Trans. Internet Technol.*, 7(2). DOI: 10.1145/1239971.1239973. 11, 12, 13

112 BIBLIOGRAPHY

Baeza-Yates, R., Castillo, C., Marin, M., and Rodriguez, A. (2005). Crawling a country: better strategies than breadth-first for web page ordering. In *Special interest tracks and posters of the 14th International Conference on World Wide Web*, WWW '05, pages 864–872, New York, NY, USA. ACM. DOI: 10.1145/1062745.1062768. 30

Bar-Yossef, Z., Broder, A. Z., Kumar, R., and Tomkins, A. (2004). Sic transit gloria telae: towards an understanding of the web's decay. In *Proceedings of the 13th International Conference on World Wide Web*, WWW '04, pages 328–337, New York, NY, USA. ACM. DOI: 10.1145/988672.988716. 11

Bar-Yossef, Z. and Gurevich, M. (2006). Random sampling from a search engine's index. In *Proceedings of WWW 2006*, pages 367–376, Edinburgh. DOI: 10.1145/1411509.1411514. 17, 18

Bar-Yossef, Z. and Rajagopalan, S. (2002). Template detection via data mining and its applications. In *In Proceedings of the 11th International Conference on World Wide Web*, pages 580–591. DOI: 10.1145/511446.511522. 50

Barabási, A.-L. and Bonabeau, E. (2003). Scale-free networks. *Scientific American*, 288(5):60–69. DOI: 10.1038/scientificamerican0503-60. 8

Baroni, M. and Bernardini, S. (2004). BootCaT: Bootstrapping corpora and terms from the web. In *Proceedings of LREC 04*, pages 1313–1316. 16

Baroni, M. and Bernardini, S., editors (2006). *WaCky! Working papers on the Web as Corpus*. GEDIT, Bologna. 115, 126

Baroni, M., Bernardini, S., Ferraresi, A., and Zanchetta, E. (2009). The WaCky Wide Web: A collection of very large linguistically processed web-crawled corpora. *Language Resources and Evaluation*, 43(3):209–226. DOI: 10.1007/s10579-009-9081-4. xiii, 3, 12, 26, 28, 50, 51, 56

Baroni, M., Chantree, F., Kilgarriff, A., and Sharoff, S. (2008). CleanEval: A competition for cleaning webpages. In *Proceedings of LREC 06*, pages 638–643, Marrakech. ELRA. 50, 51

Bauer, D., Degen, J., Deng, X., Herger, P., Gasthaus, J., Giesbrecht, E., Jansen, L., Kalina, C., Krüger, T., Märtin, R., Schmidt, M., Scholler, S., Steger, J., Stemle, E., and Evert, S. (2007). Filtering the internet by automatic subtree classification. In Fairon et al. [2007], pages 111–122. 51, 55

Baykan, E., Henzinger, M., Marian, L., and Weber, I. (2009). Purely URL-based topic classification. In *Proceedings of the 18th International Conference on World Wide Web*, pages 1109–1110. DOI: 10.1145/1526709.1526880. 35

Baykan, E., Henzinger, M., and Weber, I. (2008). Web page language identification based on URLs. In *Proceedings of the VLDB Endowment*, pages 176–187. 35

Becchetti, L., Castillo, C., Donato, D., and Fazzone, A. (2006). A comparison of sampling techniques for Web characterization. In *Proceedings of the Workshop on Link Analysis 2006 (LinkKDD)*. ACM Press. 28

Berger, A. L., Della Pietra, S. A., and Della Pietra, V. J. (1996). A maximum entropy approach to natural language processing. *Computational Linguistics*, 22(1):39–71. 68

Berners-Lee, T. (1989). Information management: A proposal. Technical report, W3C. 8

Best, K.-H. (2001). Probability distributions of language entities. *Journal of Quantitative Linguistics*, 8(1):1–11. DOI: 10.1076/jqul.8.1.1.4091. 86

Best, K.-H. (2005). Satzlänge. In Köhler, R., Altmann, G., and Piotrowski, R. G., editors, *Quantitative Linguistik. Ein Internationales Handbuch*, volume 27 of *Handbücher zur Sprach- und Kommunikationswissenschaft*, chapter 22, pages 298–304. de Gruyter, Berlin/New York. 86

Bharat, K. and Broder, A. (1998). A technique for measuring the relative size and overlap of public web search engines. In *Proceedings of the 7th International World Wide Web Conference*, pages 379–388. Elsevier Science. DOI: 10.1016/S0169-7552(98)00127-5. 17

Biber, D. (1993). Representativeness in corpus design. *Literary and Linguistic Computing*, 8(4):243–257. DOI: 10.1093/llc/8.4.243. 106, 108

Biber, D. and Kurjian, J. (2007). Towards a taxonomy of web registers an text types: a multidimensional analysis. In Hundt et al. [2007], pages 109–131. 106

Biemann, C., Bildhauer, F., Evert, S., Goldhahn, D., Quasthoff, U., Schäfer, R., and Zesch, T. (in prep.). Scalable construction of high-quality web corpora. *Special issue of Journal for Language Technology and Computational Linguistics*. 105

Biemann, C., Heyer, G., Quasthoff, U., and Richter, M. (2007). The Leipzig Corpora Collection - Monolingual corpora of standard size. In *Proceedings of Corpus Linguistics 2007*, Birmingham, UK. xiii, 3, 86

Bird, S., Loper, E., and Klein, E. (2009). *Natural Language Processing with Python*. O'Reilly, Sebastopol, Calif. 84

Björneborn, L. and Ingwersen, P. (2004). Toward a basic framework for Webometrics. *J. Am. Soc. Inf. Sci.*, 55(14):1216–1227. DOI: 10.1002/asi.20077. 11

Bloem, J., Regneri, M., and Thater, S. (2012). Robust processing of noisy web-collected data. In Jancsary, J., editor, *Proceedings of KONVENS 2012*, pages 189–193. ÖGAI. 78

Bloom, B. (1970). Space/time trade-offs in hash coding with allowable errors. *Communications of ACM*, 13(7):422–426. DOI: 10.1145/362686.362692. 21

Brants, S., Dipper, S., Hansen, S., Lezius, W., and Smith, G. (2002). The TIGER treebank. In *Proceedings of the Workshop on Treebanks and Linguistic Theories*, Sozopol. 75

Brants, T. (2000). TnT – a statistical part-of-speech tagger. In *ANLP*, pages 224–231. DOI: 10.3115/974147.974178. 75

Brill, E. (1992). A simple rule-based part of speech tagger. In *Proceedings of the workshop on Speech and Natural Language*, HLT '91, pages 112–116, Stroudsburg, PA, USA. Association for Computational Linguistics. DOI: 10.3115/1075527.1075553. 68

Brill, E. (1995). Transformation-based error-driven learning and natural language processing: a case study in part-of-speech tagging. *Computational Linguistics*, 21(4):543–565. 68

Brin, S. and Page, L. (1998). The anatomy of a large-scale hypertextual web search engine. In *Proceedings of the 7th International World Wide Web Conference*, pages 107–117. Elsevier Science. 2, 32

Broder, A., Kumar, R., Maghoul, F., Raghavan, P., Stata, R., Tomkins, A., and Wiener, J. L. (2000). Graph structure in the web. In *Proceedings of the 9th International World Wide Web conference on Computer Networks: The International Journal of Computer and Telecommunications Networking*, pages 309–320. North-Holland Publishing Co. DOI: 10.1016/S1389-1286(00)00083-9. 9

Broder, A. and Mitzenmacher, M. (2004). Network applications of Bloom filters: A survey. *Internet Mathematics*, 1(4):485–509. DOI: 10.1080/15427951.2004.10129096. 21

Broder, A. Z., Glassman, S. C., Manasse, M. S., and Zweig, G. (1997). Syntactic clustering of the Web. Technical Note 1997-115, SRC, Palo Alto. 60, 61

Bryan, K. and Leise, T. (2006). The $25,000,000,000 eigenvector: The linear algebra behind Google. *SIAM Review*, 48(3):569–581. DOI: 10.1137/050623280. 32

Cai, D., Yu, S., Wen, J., and Ma, W. (2003). Extracting content structure for web pages based on visual representation. In *Proceedings of the 5th Asia-Pacific Web Conference on Web Technologies and Applications*, pages 406–417. DOI: 10.1007/3-540-36901-5_42. 50

Calzolari, N., Choukri, K., Declerck, T., Doğan, M. U., Maegaard, B., Mariani, J., Odijk, J., and Piperidis, S., editors (2012). *Proceedings of the Eight International Conference on Language Resources and Evaluation (LREC'12)*, Istanbul. ELRA. 118, 123, 125

Carter, S., Weerkamp, W., and Tsagkias, M. (2012). Microblog language identification: overcoming the limitations of short, unedited and idiomatic text. *Language Resources and Evaluation*, pages 1–21. DOI: 10.1007/s10579-012-9195-y. 57

Castillo, C. and Davison, B. D. (2011). *Adversarial Web Search*, volume 4(5) of *Foundations and Trends in Information Retrieval*. now Publishers, Hanover, MA. 15

Cavnar, W. B. and Trenkle, J. M. (1994). N-gram-based text categorization. In *Proceedings of SDAIR-94, 3rd Annual Symposium on Document Analysis and Information Retrieval*, pages 161–175. 57

Chakrabarti, D., Kumar, R., and Punera, K. (2007). Page-level template detection via isotonic smoothing. In *Proceedings of the 16th International Conference on World Wide Web*, pages 61–70. DOI: 10.1145/1242572.1242582. 50

Chakrabarti, S., Dom, B., and Indyk, P. (1998). Enhanced hypertext categorization using hyperlinks. In *Proceedings of the 1998 ACM SIGMOD International Conference on Management of data*, SIGMOD '98, pages 307–318. ACM. DOI: 10.1145/276304.276332. 35

Chakrabarti, S., van den Berg, M., and Dom, B. (1999). Focused crawling: a new approach to topic-specific web resource discovery. *Computer Networks*, 31:1623–1640. DOI: 10.1016/S1389-1286(99)00052-3. 35

Chen, K.-J. and Liu, S.-H. (1992). Word identification for Mandarin Chinese sentences. In *COLING*, pages 101–107. DOI: 10.3115/992066.992085. 66

Cho, J., García-Molina, H., and Page, L. (1998). Efficient crawling through URL ordering. In *Proceedings of the 7th International World Wide Web Conference*. DOI: 10.1016/S0169-7552(98)00108-1. 35

Cho, J. and Schonfeld, U. (2007). Rankmass crawler: A crawler with high personalized PageRank coverage guarantee. In *Proceedings of the 33rd International Conference on Very Large Data Bases*. 30

Church, K. W. and Gale, W. A. (1995). Poisson mixtures. *Natural Language Engineering*, 1(2):163–190. DOI: 10.1017/S1351324900000139. 95

Church, K. W. and Mercer, R. L. (1993). Introduction to the special issue on computational linguistics using large corpora. *Computational Linguistics*, 19(1):1–24. 69

Ciaramita, M. and Baroni, M. (2006). Measuring web-corpus randomness: A progress report. In Baroni and Bernardini [2006], pages 127–158. 18, 31, 107

Clark, A. (2003). Pre-processing very noisy text. In *Proceedings of the Workshop on Shallow Processing of Large Corpora (SProLaC 2003), 27 March, 2003*, pages 12–22. 81

Clark, E. and Araki, K. (2011). Text normalization in social media: progress, problems and applications for a pre-processing system of casual English. *Procedia - Social and Behavioral Sciences*, 27:2–11. DOI: 10.1016/j.sbspro.2011.10.577. 81

Cook, P. and Hirst, G. (2012). Do web-corpora from top-level domains represent national varieties of English? In *Proceedings of the 11th International Conference on the Statistical Analysis of Textual Data*, pages 281–293, Liège. 13

Cucerzan, S. and Brill, E. (2004). Spelling correction as an iterative process that exploits the collective knowledge of web users. In *EMNLP*, pages 293–300. ACL. 2, 79

Curran, J. R. and Moens, M. (2002). Scaling context space. In *Proceedings of the 40th Annual Meeting on Association for Computational Linguistics*, ACL '02, pages 231–238. DOI: 10.3115/1073083.1073123. 105

Damerau, F. J. (1964). A technique for computer detection and correction of spelling errors. *Communications of the ACM*, 7(3):171–176. DOI: 10.1145/363958.363994. 80

Damerau, F. J. (1993). Generating and evaluating domain-oriented multi-word terms from texts. *Information Processing & Management*, 29(4):433–447. DOI: 10.1016/0306-4573(93)90039-G. 99

Davies, M. (2002). Corpus del español: 100 million words, 1200s-1900s. 2

Dunning, T. (1994). Statistical identification of language. Technical Report MCCS-94-273, Computing Research Laboratory, New Mexico State University. 57

Eckart, T., Quasthoff, U., and Goldhahn, D. (2012). The influence of corpus quality on statistical measurements on language resources. In *Proceedings of LREC 08*, pages 2318–2321, Istanbul. 86

Edmundson, H. P. and Wyllys, R. E. (1961). Automatic abstracting and indexing. Survey and recommendations. *Communications of the ACM*, 4(5):226–234. DOI: 10.1145/366532.366545. 99

Esakov, J., Lopresti, D. P., and Sandberg, J. S. (1994). Classification and distribution of optical character recognition errors. In *Proceedings of the IS&T/SPIE International Symposium on Electronic Imaging*, volume 2181, pages 204–216. DOI: 10.1117/12.171108. 72

Eu, J. (2008). Testing search engine frequencies: Patterns of inconsistency. *Corpus Linguistics and Linguistic Theory*, 4(2):177–207. DOI: 10.1515/CLLT.2008.008. 3

Evert, S. (2007). StupidOS: A high-precision approach to boilerplate removal. In Fairon et al. [2007], pages 123–134. 51, 55

Fairon, C., Naets, H., Kilgarriff, A., and de Schryver, G.-M., editors (2007). *Building and Exploring Web Corpora: Proceedings of the 3rd Web as Corpus Workshop (Incorporating CLEANEVAL)*, Louvain. Presses universitaires de Louvain. 112, 116, 117, 118, 119, 122, 125

Faruqui, M. and Padó, S. (2010). Training and evaluating a German named entity recognizer with semantic generalization. In *Proceedings of KONVENS 2010*, Saarbrücken, Germany. 105

Ferraresi, A., Bernardini, S., Picci, G., and Baroni, M. (2008). Web corpora for bilingual lexicography: A pilot study of English/French collocation extraction and translation. In *Proceedings of UCCTS: International Symposium on Using Corpora in Contrastive and Translation Studies*. 105

Fetterly, D., Craswell, N., and Vinay, V. (2009). The impact of crawl policy on web search effectiveness. In *Proceedings of the 32nd International ACM SIGIR Conference on Research and Development in Information Retrieval*, SIGIR '09, pages 580–587, New York, NY, USA. ACM. DOI: 10.1145/1571941.1572041. 30

Fetterly, D., Manasse, M., Najork, M., and Wiener, J. (2003). A large-scale study of the evolution of web pages. In *Proceedings of the 12th International Conference on World Wide Web*. DOI: 10.1145/775152.775246. 11

Fitschen, A. and Gupta, P. (2008). Lemmatising and morphological tagging. In Lüdeling and Kytö [2008], pages 552–564. 69

Fletcher, W. H. (2011). Corpus analysis of the World Wide Web. In Chapelle, C. A., editor, *Encyclopedia of Applied Linguistics*. Wiley-Blackwell, Hoboken. xiii, 72

Gao, W. and Abou-Assaleh, T. (2007). GenieKnows web page cleaning system. In Fairon et al. [2007], pages 135–140. 50, 51

Geyken, A. (2006). The DWDS corpus: A reference corpus for the German language of the 20th Century. In Fellbaum, C. D., editor, *Collocations and Idioms: Linguistic, Lexicographic, and Computational Aspects*, pages 23–40. Continuum Press, London. 1

Giesbrecht, E. and Evert, S. (2009). Part-of-speech (POS) tagging – a solved task? An evaluation of POS taggers for the German Web as Corpus. In Alegria, I., Leturia, I., and Sharoff, S., editors, *Proceedings of the Fifth Web as Corpus Workshop (WAC5)*, pages 27–35, San Sebastián. 75, 79, 83, 104

Gillick, D. (2009). Sentence boundary detection and the problem with the U.S. In *Proceedings of Human Language Technologies: The 2009 Annual Conference of the North American Chapter of the Association for Computational Linguistics, Companion Volume: Short Papers*, pages 241–244, Stroudsburg, PA, USA. Association for Computational Linguistics. 84

Giménez, J. and Màrquez, L. (2003). Fast and accurate part-of-speech tagging: The SVM approach revisited. In Nicolov, N., Bontcheva, K., Angelova, G., and Mitkov, R., editors, *RANLP*, pages 153–163. John Benjamins, Amsterdam/Philadelphia. DOI: 10.1162/coli.2000.27.4.603b. 69

Giménez, J. and Màrquez, L. (2004). SVMTool. a general POS tagger generator based on Support Vector Machines. In Lino, M. T., Xavier, M. F., Ferreira, F., Costa, R., and Silva, R., editors, *Proceedings of the 4th International Conference on Language Ressources and Evaluation (LREC 2004)*, pages 43–46, Lisbon, Portugal. 75

Girardi, C. (2007). Htmcleaner: Extracting the relevant text from the web pages. In Fairon et al. [2007], pages 141–144. 51

Gjoka, M., Kurant, M., Butts, C. T., and Markopoulou, A. (2011). A walk in Facebook: a case study of unbiased sampling of Facebook. In *Proceedings of IEEE INFOCOM 2010*, San Diego. IEEE. DOI: 10.1109/INFCOM.2010.5462078. 29, 31

Goldhahn, D., Eckart, T., and Quasthoff, U. (2012). Building large monolingual dictionaries at the Leipzig Corpora Collection: From 100 to 200 languages. In Calzolari et al. [2012]. xiii, 86

Goldsmith, J. A. (2010). Segmentation and morphology. In Clark, A., Fox, C., and Lappin, S., editors, *The handbook of computational linguistics and natural language processing*, pages 364–393. Wiley-Backwell, Chichester. DOI: 10.1002/9781444324044. 66, 69

Gomes, D. and Silva, M. J. (2005). Characterizing a national community web. *ACM Trans. Internet Technol.*, 5(3):508–531. DOI: 10.1145/1084772.1084775. 35

Gottron, T. and Lipka, N. (2010). A comparison of language identification approaches on short, query-style texts. In Gurrin, C., He, Y., Kazai, G., Kruschwitz, U., Little, S., Roelleke, T., Rüger, S., and Rijsbergen, K., editors, *Advances in Information Retrieval*, volume 5993 of *Lecture Notes in Computer Science*, pages 611–614. Springer Berlin Heidelberg. 57

Graff, D. and Cieri, C. (2003). English Gigaword. Linguistic Data Consortium, Philadelphia. 104

Grefenstette, G. (1995). Comparing two language identification schemes. In *Proceedings of the 3rd Internation conference on Statistical Analysis of Textual Data (JADT 1995)*, pages 263–268, Rome. 57

Grefenstette, G. and Tapanainen, P. (1994). What is a word? What is a sentence? In *Proceedings of 3rd Conference on Computational Lexicography and Text Research*. 45, 67

Gries, S. (2008). Dispersions and adjusted frequencies in corpora. *International Journal of Corpus Linguistics*, 13(4):403–437. DOI: 10.1075/ijcl.13.4.02gri. 103

Grzybek, P. (2007). History and methodology of word length studies. In Grzybek, P., editor, *Contributions to the science of text and language. Word length studies and related issues*, pages 15–90. Springer, Dordrecht. 86

Gulli, A. and Signorini, A. (2005). The indexable web is more than 11.5 billion pages. In *Special interest tracks and posters of the 14th International Conference on World Wide Web*, WWW '05, pages 902–903, New York, NY, USA. ACM. DOI: 10.1145/1062745.1062789. 16

Guo, J., Xu, G., Li, H., and Cheng, X. (2008). A unified and discriminative model for query refinement. In *Proceedings of the 31st Annual International ACM SIGIR Conference on Research and Development in Information Retrieval*, SIGIR '08, pages 379–386, New York, NY, USA. ACM. DOI: 10.1145/1390334.1390400. 3

Hagen, M., Potthast, M., Stein, B., and Bräutigam, C. (2011). Query segmentation revisited. In *Proceedings of the 20th International Conference on World Wide Web*, WWW '11, pages 97–106, New York, NY, USA. ACM. DOI: 10.1145/1963405.1963423. 3

Hall, M., Frank, E., Holmes, G., Pfahringer, B., Reutemann, P., and Witten, I. H. (2009). The WEKA data mining software: An update. *SIGKDD Explorations*, 11(1):10–18. DOI: 10.1145/1656274.1656278. 55

Hall, M. and Witten, I. H. (2011). *Data mining: practical machine learning tools and techniques*. Kaufmann, Burlington. 55

Henzinger, M. (2006). Finding nearduplicate web pages: A largescale evaluation of algorithms. In *Proceedings of the 29th Annual International ACM SIGIR Conference on Research and Development in Information Retrieval*, pages 284–291. DOI: 10.1145/1148170.1148222. 61

Henzinger, M. R., Heydon, A., Mitzenmacher, M., and Najork, M. (2000). On near-uniform URL sampling. In *Proceedings of the 9th International World Wide Web Conference on Computer Networks: The International Journal of Computer and Telecommunications Networking*, pages 295–308. North-Holland Publishing Co. DOI: 10.1016/S1389-1286(00)00055-4. 31, 32

Hoffmann, K. and Weerkamp, W. (2007). Web corpus cleaning using content and structure. In Fairon et al. [2007], pages 145–154. 51, 55

Hofland, K. and Johansson, S. (1982). *Word frequencies in British and American English*. The Norwegian Computing Centre for the Humanities, Bergen. 99

Huang, C.-R., Šimon, P., Hsieh, S.-K., and Prévot, L. (2007). Rethinking Chinese word segmentation: tokenization, character classification, or wordbreak identification. In *Proceedings of the 45th Annual Meeting of the ACL on Interactive Poster and Demonstration Sessions*, ACL '07, pages 69–72, Stroudsburg, PA, USA. Association for Computational Linguistics. DOI: 10.3115/1557769.1557791. 66

Hundt, M., Nesselhauf, N., and Biewer, C., editors (2007). *Corpus linguistics and the web*. Rodopi, Amsterdam and New York. 113, 121, 122

Hunston, S. (2008). Collection strategies and design decisions. In Lüdeling and Kytö [2008], pages 154–168. 108

Issac, F. (2007). Yet another web crawler. In Fairon, C., Naets, H., Kilgarriff, A., and de Schryver, G.-M., editors, *Proceedings of the 3rd Web as Corpus Workshop (WAC 3) – Building and Exploring Web Corpora*, pages 57–68, Louvain. Presses universitaires de Louvain. 31, 51

Keller, F. and Lapata, M. (2003). Using the web to obtain frequencies for unseen bigrams. *Computational Linguistics*, 29(3):459–484. 3

Kilgarriff, A. (2001). Comparing corpora. *International Journal of Corpus Linguistics*, 6(1):97–133. DOI: 10.1075/ijcl.6.1.05kil. 93, 95, 96, 97, 99

Kilgarriff, A. (2006). Googleology is bad science. *Computational Linguistics*, 33(1):147–151. DOI: 10.1162/coli.2007.33.1.147. 2

Kilgarriff, A. (2009). Simple maths for keywords. In *Proceedings of the Corpus Linguistics Conference*, Liverpool. 13

Kilgarriff, A. (2012). Getting to know your corpus. In Sojka, P., Horák, A., Kopeček, I., and Pala, K., editors, *Text, Speech and Dialogue - 15th International Conference, TSD 2012, Brno, Czech Republic, September 3-7, 2012. Proceedings*, pages 3–15, Heidelberg. Springer. DOI: 10.1007/978-3-642-23538-2. 99

Kilgarriff, A., Baisa, V., Jakubicek, M., Kovara, V., and Rychly, P. (in prep.). How to evaluate a corpus. ms. 104, 105

Kilgarriff, A. and Grefenstette, G. (2003). Introduction to the special issue on the Web as corpus. *Computational Linguistics*, 29:333–347. DOI: 10.1162/089120103322711569. xiii

Kiss, T. and Strunk, J. (2006). Unsupervised multilingual sentence boundary detection. *Computational Linguistics*, 34(4):485–525. DOI: 10.1162/coli.2006.32.4.485. 67, 68

Kohlschütter, C., Fankhauser, P., and Nejdl, W. (2010). Boilerplate detection using shallow text features. In *Proceedings of the third ACM International Conference on Web Search and Data Mining*, pages 441–450. DOI: 10.1145/1718487.1718542. 51

Kornai, A. and Hálacsy, P. (2008). Google for the linguist on a budget. In Evert, S., Kilgarriff, A., and Sharoff, S., editors, *Proceedings of the 4th Web as Corpus Workshop (WAC-4) – Can we beat Google?*, pages 8–11, Marrakech. 30, 31

Korpela, J. K. (2006). *Unicode Explained*. O'Reilly Media, Sebastopol. 42

Kukich, K. (1992). Techniques for automatically correcting words in text. *ACM Computing Surveys*, 24(4):377–439. DOI: 10.1145/146370.146380. 72, 78, 79, 80

Kullback, S. and Leibler, R. A. (1951). On information and sufficiency. *The Annals of Mathematical Statistics*, 22(1):79–86. DOI: 10.1214/aoms/1177729694. 107

Kupietz, M., Belica, C., Keibel, H., and Witt, A. (2010). The German reference corpus DeReKo: A primordial sample for linguistic research. In Calzolari, N., Choukri, K., Maegaard, B., Mariani, J., Odijk, J., Piperidis, S., Rosner, M., and Tapias, D., editors, *Proceedings of the Seventh International Conference on Language Resources and Evaluation (LREC'10)*, pages 1848–1854, Valletta, Malta. European Language Resources Association (ELRA). 1, 28

Kurant, M., Markopoulou, A., and Thiran, P. (2010). On the bias of BFS (Breadth First Search). In *International Teletraffic Congress (ITC 22)*. DOI: 10.1109/ITC.2010.5608727. 30

Kurant, M., Gjoka, M., Butts, C. T., and Markopoulou, A. (2011). Walking on a graph with a magnifying glass: stratified sampling via weighted random walks. In *Proceedings of the ACM SIGMETRICS Joint International Conference on Measurement and Modeling of Computer Systems*, SIGMETRICS '11, pages 281–292, New York, NY, USA. ACM. DOI: 10.1145/1993744.1993773. 30

Lafferty, J. D., McCallum, A., and Pereira, F. C. N. (2001). Conditional Random Fields: Probabilistic models for segmenting and labeling sequence data. In *Proceedings of the Eighteenth International Conference on Machine Learning*, ICML '01, pages 282–289, San Francisco, CA, USA. Morgan Kaufmann Publishers Inc. 68

Landauer, T. K., Foltz, P. W., and Laham, D. (1998). Introduction to Latent Semantic Analysis. *Discourse Processes*, 25:259–84. DOI: 10.1080/01638539809545028. 56

Leech, G. (1993). 100 Million words of English. *English Today*, 9(1):9–15. DOI: 10.1017/S0266078400006854. 1, 13

Leech, G. (2007). New resources or just better old ones? The Holy Grail of representativeness. In Hundt et al. [2007], pages 133–149. 108

Levenshtein, V. I. (1966). Binary codes capable of correcting deletions, insertions, and reversals. *Soviet Physics Doklady*, 10(8):707–710. 80

Li, M., Zhu, M., Zhang, Y., and Zhou, M. (2006). Exploring distributional similarity based models for query spelling correction. In Calzolari, N., Cardie, C., and Isabelle, P., editors, *ACL 2006, 21st International Conference on Computational Linguistics and 44th Annual Meeting of the Association for Computational Linguistics, Proceedings of the Conference, Sydney, Australia, 17–21 July 2006*. The Association for Computer Linguistics. 79

Liu, V. and Curran, J. R. (2006). Web text corpus for natural language processing. In *11th Conference of the European Chapter of the Association for Computational Linguistics: EACL 2006*, pages 233–240. 71, 104, 105

Lopresti, D. (2009). Optical character recognition errors and their effects on natural language processing. *International Journal on Document Analysis and Recognition*, 12(3):141–151. DOI: 10.1145/1390749.1390753. 72

Lüdeling, A., Evert, S., and Baroni, M. (2007). Using the web for linguistic purposes. In Hundt et al. [2007], pages 7–24. xiii

Lüdeling, A. and Kytö, M., editors (2008). *Corpus linguistics: an International Handbook*. Walter de Gruyter, Berlin. DOI: 10.1515/9783110211429. 117, 120, 125

MacIntyre, R. (1995). Sed script to produce Penn Treebank tokenization on arbitrary raw text. `http://www.cis.upenn.edu/~treebank/tokenization.html`. 67

Madhavan, J., Afanasiev, L., Antova, L., and Halevy, A. (2009). Harnessing the Deep Web: Present and Future. In *4th Biennial Conference on Innovative Data Systems Research (CIDR)*. 10

Maiya, A. S. and Berger-Wolf, T. Y. (2011). Benefits of bias: towards better characterization of network sampling. In *Proceedings of the 17th ACM SIGKDD International Conference on Knowledge Discovery and Data Mining*, KDD '11, pages 105–113, New York, NY, USA. ACM. DOI: 10.1145/2020408.2020431. 25, 30

Manning, C., Raghavan, P., and Schütze, H. (2009). *An Introduction to Information Retrieval*. CUP, Cambridge. 2, 7, 8, 20, 32, 61, 104

Manning, C. D. and Schütze, H. (1999). *Foundations of statistical natural language processing*. MIT Press, Cambridge, MA. 68, 97

Marcus, M. P., Santorini, B., and Marcinkiewicz, M. A. (1993). Building a large annotated corpus of English: The Penn Treebank. *Computational Linguistics*, 19(2):313–330. 1, 78

Marcus, M. P., Santorini, B., Marcinkiewicz, M. A., and Taylor, A. (1999). Treebank-3. Technical report, Linguistic Data Consortium, Philadelphia. 1

Marek, M., Pecina, P., and Spousta, M. (2007). Web page cleaning with Conditional Random Fields. In Fairon et al. [2007], pages 155–162. 51, 55

McEnery, T., Xiao, R., and Tono, Y. (2006). *Corpus-based language studies. An advanced resource book*. Routledge, London and New York. 108

Mehler, A., Sharoff, S., and Santini, M., editors (2010). *Genres on the web. Computational models and empirical studies*, volume 42 of *Text, Speech and Language Technology*. Springer, Dordrecht. 106, 126

Menczer, F., Pant, G., and Srinivasan, P. (2004). Topical web crawlers: Evaluating adaptive algorithms. *ACM Trans. Internet Technol.*, 4(4):378–419. DOI: 10.1145/1031114.1031117. 35

Mikheev, A. (2002). Periods, Capitalized Words, etc. *Computational Linguistics*, 28(3):289–318. DOI: 10.1162/089120102760275992. 67

Mikheev, A. (2003). Text segmentation. In Mitkov [2003], chapter 10, pages 201–218. 68

Mitkov, R., editor (2003). *The Oxford handbook of computational linguistics*. Oxford University Press, Oxford. 123, 127

Mohr, G., Stack, M., Ranitovic, I., Avery, D., and Kimpton, M. (2004). Introduction to Heritrix, an archival quality web crawler. In *Proceedings of the 4th International Web Archiving Workshop (IWAW'04)*. 22, 29

Müller, F. H. (2004). Stylebook for the Tübingen partially parsed corpus of written German (TüPP-D/Z). Technical report, Seminar für Sprachwissenschaft, Universität Tübingen. 105

Najork, M. and Wiener, J. L. (2001). Breadth-first crawling yields high-quality pages. In *Proceedings of the 10th Conference on World Wide Web*, pages 114–118. Elsevier Science. DOI: 10.1145/371920.371965. 30

Odell, M. K. and Russell, R. C. (1918). U.S. Patents 1261167 (1918), 1435663 (1922). 80

Olston, C. and Najork, M. (2010). *Web Crawling*, volume 4(3) of *Foundations and Trends in Information Retrieval*. now Publishers, Hanover, MA. 7, 16, 35

Ostendorf, M., Favre, B., Grishman, R., Hakkani-Tur, D., Harper, M., Hillard, D., Hirschberg, J., Ji, H., Kahn, J. G., Liu, Y., Maskey, S., Matusov, E., Ney, H., Rosenberg, A., Shriberg, E., Wang, W., and Wooters, C. (2007). Speech segmentation and its impact on spoken document processing. Manuscript, Signal Processing Magazine. 72

Padró, L. and Stanilovsky, E. (2012). Freeling 3.0: Towards wider multilinguality. In Calzolari et al. [2012], pages 2473–2479. 83

Pagh, A., Pagh, R., and Rao, S. S. (2005). An optimal Bloom filter replacement. In *Proceedings of the Sixteenth Annual ACM-SIAM Symposium on Discrete Algorithms*, pages 823–829. DOI: 10.1145/1070432.1070548. 21

Palmer, D. D. and Hearst, M. A. (1997). Adaptive multilingual sentence boundary disambiguation. *Computational Linguistics*, 23(2):241–267. 67, 68

Pasternack, J. and Roth, D. (2009). Extracting article text from the web with maximum subsequence segmentation. In *Proceedings of the 18th International Conference on World Wide Web*, pages 971–980. DOI: 10.1145/1526709.1526840. 51, 55

Peterson, J. L. (1986). A note on undetected typing errors. *Communications of the ACM*, 29(7):633–637. DOI: 10.1145/6138.6146. 78

Philips, L. (1990). Hanging on the metaphone. *Computer Language Magazine*, 7(12):38–44. 80

Pomikálek, J. (2011). *Removing boilerplate and duplicate content from web corpora*. PhD thesis, Masaryk University Faculty of Informatics, Brno. 50, 51

Pomikálek, J., Jakubíček, M., and Rychlý, P. (2012). Building a 70 billion word corpus of English from ClueWeb. In *Proceedings of LREC 08*, pages 502–506. 20

Porter, M. F. (1980). An algorithm for suffix stripping. *Program*, 14(3):130–137. DOI: 10.1108/eb046814. 69

Postel, J. (1969). Die Kölner Phonetik. Ein Verfahren zur Identifizierung von Personennamen auf der Grundlage der Gestaltanalyse. *IBM-Nachrichten*, 19:925–931. 80

Rabin, M. O. (1981). Fingerprinting by random polynomials. Technical Report TR-CSE-03-01, Center for Research in Computing Technology, Harvard University, Harvard. 63

Ratnaparkhi, A. (1998). Maximum entropy models for natural language ambiguity resolution. IRCS Tech Report IRCS-98-15, University of Pennsylvania, Institute for Research in Cognitive Science. 68

Rayson, P. (2003). *Matrix: A statistical method and software tool for linguistic analysis through corpus comparison*. PhD thesis, Lancaster University. 103

Rayson, P., Charles, O., and Auty, I. (2012). Can Google count? Estimating search engine result consistency. In Kilgarriff, A. and Sharoff, S., editors, *Proceedings of the seventh Web as Corpus Workshop*, pages 23–30. 3

Rehm, G., Santini, M., Mehler, A., Braslavski, P., Gleim, R., Stubbe, A., Symonenko, S., Tavosanis, M., and Vidulin, V. (2008). Towards a reference corpus of web genres for the evaluation of genre identification systems. In Calzolari, N., Choukri, K., Maegaard, B., Mariani, J., Odjik, J., Piperidis, S., and Tapias, D., editors, *Proceedings of the Sixth International Conference on Language Resources and Evaluation (LREC'08)*, Marrakech, Morocco. European Language Resources Association (ELRA) 106

Řehůřek, R. and Kolkus, M. (2009). Language identification on the web: Extending the dictionary method. In Gelbukh, A., editor, *Computational Linguistics and Intelligent Text Processing*, volume 5449 of *Lecture Notes in Computer Science*, pages 357–368. Springer Berlin Heidelberg. 58

Risvik, K. M., Mikołjewski, T., and Boros, P. (2003). Query segmentation for web search. In *Proceedings of the 12th International Conference on World Wide Web*, WWW '03, New York, NY, USA. ACM. 3

Rusmevichientong, P., Pennock, D. M., Lawrence, S., and Giles, C. L. (2001). Methods for sampling pages uniformly from the World Wide Web. In *AAAI Fall Symposium on Using Uncertainty Within Computation*, pages 121–128. 31, 34

Safran, M., Althagafi, A., and Che, D. (2012). Improving relevance prediction for focused Web crawlers. In *IEEE/ACIS 11th International Conference on Computer and Information Science (ICIS), 2012*, pages 161–166. DOI: 10.1109/ICIS.2012.61. 35

Saralegi, X. and Leturia, I. (2007). Kimatu, a tool for cleaning non-content text parts from HTML docs. In Fairon et al. [2007], pages 163–167. 51

Schiller, A., Teufel, S., Stöckert, C., and Thielen, C. (1999). *Guidelines für das Tagging deutscher Textkorpora mit STTS (kleines und großes Tagset)*. Institut für maschinelle Sprachverarbeitung, Universität Stuttgart and Institut für Sprachwissenschaft, Universität Tübingen, Stuttgart and Tübingen. 79

Schmid, H. (1994a). Part-of-speech tagging with neural networks. In *COLING*, pages 172–176. DOI: 10.3115/991886.991915. 68

Schmid, H. (1994b). Probabilistic part-of-speech tagging using decision trees. In *Proceedings of International Conference on New Methods in Language Processing*. DOI: 10.1007/BFb0026668. 67, 68

Schmid, H. (1995). Improvements in part-of-speech tagging with an application to German. In *Proceedings of the EACL SIGDAT-Workshop*, Dublin, Ireland. DOI: 10.1007/978-94-017-2390-9_2. 75, 83

Schmid, H. (2000). Unsupervised learning of period disambiguation for tokenisation. Internal report, IMS, Universität Stuttgart. 67, 68, 72

Schmid, H. (2008). Tokenizing and part-of-speech tagging. In Lüdeling and Kytö [2008], pages 527–551. 74

Schäfer, R. and Bildhauer, F. (2012). Building large corpora from the web using a new efficient tool chain. In Calzolari et al. [2012], pages 486–493. 12, 20, 26, 28, 51, 55, 56

Schäfer, R. and Sayatz, U. (submitted). Die Kurzformen des Indefinitartikels im Deutschen. 76

Scott, M. (1997). PC analysis of key words - and key key words. *System*, 25(2):233–245. DOI: 10.1016/S0346-251X(97)00011-0. 99, 103

Scott, M. (2001). Comparing corpora and identifying keywords, collocations, frequency distributions through the WordSmith Tools suite of computer programs. In Ghadessy, M., Henry, A., and Roseberry, R., editors, *Small Corpus Studies and ELT*, pages 47–67. Benjamins, Amsterdam and Philadelphia. 99, 102

Sebastiani, F. (2002). Machine learning in automated text categorization. *ACM Computing Surveys*, 34(1):1–47. DOI: 10.1145/505282.505283. 106

Serrano, M. A., Maguitman, A., Boguñá, M., Fortunato, S., and Vespignani, A. (2007). Decoding the structure of the WWW: a comparative analysis of web crawls. *ACM Trans. Web*, 1(2). DOI: 10.1145/1255438.1255442. 9

Sharoff, S. (2006). Creating general-purpose corpora using automated search engine queries. In Baroni and Bernardini [2006], pages 63–98. 106

Sharoff, S. (2010). In the garden and in the jungle: comparing genres in the BNC and internet. In Mehler et al. [2010], pages 149–166. 106

Sinclair, J. (1996). Preliminary recommendations on corpus typology. Technical Report EAG–TCWG–CTYP/P, Expert Advisory Group on Language Engineering Standards document. 106

Spärck Jones, K. (1972). A statistical interpretation of term specificity and its application in retrieval. *Journal of Documentation*, 28(1):11–21. 99, 104

Spousta, M., Marek, M., and Pecina, P. (2008). Victor: The web-page cleaning tool. In Evert, S., Kilgarriff, A., and Sharoff, S., editors, *Proceedings of the 4th Web as Corpus Workshop*, pages 12–17, Marrakech. 40, 51, 52, 55

Sproat, R., Black, A. W., Chen, S., Kumar, S., Ostendorf, M., and Richards, C. (2001). Normalization of non-standard words. *Computer Speech and Language*, 15:287–333. DOI: 10.1006/csla.2001.0169. 81

Sproat, R. and Shih, C. (1990). A statistical method for finding word boundaries in Chinese text. *Computer Processing of Chinese and Oriental Languages*, 4:336–351. 66

Sproat, R., Shih, C., Gale, W., and Chang, N. (1996). A stochastic finite-state word-segmentation algorithm for Chinese. *Computational Linguistics*, 22(3):377–404. 66

Srinivasan, P., Menczer, F., and Pant, G. (2005). A general evaluation framework for topical crawlers. *Inf. Retr.*, 8(3):417–447. DOI: 10.1007/s10791-005-6993-5. 35

Subramaniam, L. V., Roy, S., Faruquie, T. A., and Negi, S. (2009). A survey of types of text noise and techniques to handle noisy text. In *Proceedings of The Third Workshop on Analytics for Noisy Unstructured Text Data*, AND '09, pages 115–122, New York, NY, USA. ACM. DOI: 10.1145/1568296.1568315. 72

Suchomel, V. and Pomikálek, J. (2012). Effcient Web crawling for large text corpora. In Kilgarriff, A. and Sharoff, S., editors, *Proceedings of the seventh Web as Corpus Workshop*, pages 40–44. 26, 35

Tapanainen, P. and Voutilainen, A. (1994). Tagging accurately: Don't guess if you know. In *Proceedings of the Fourth Conference on Applied Natural Language Processing*, ANLC '94, pages 47–52. DOI: 10.3115/974358.974370. 68, 69

Teahan, W. J. (2000). Text classification and segmentation using Minimum Cross Entropy. In *Proceeding of RIAO*, pages 943–961. 58

Teahan, W. J., McNab, R., Wen, Y., and Witten, I. H. (2000). A compression-based algorithm for Chinese word segmentation. *Computational Linguistics*, 26(3):375–393. DOI: 10.1162/089120100561746. 66

Thelwall, M. (2009). Introduction to Webometrics: quantitative web research for the social sciences. *Synthesis Lectures on Information Concepts, Retrieval, and Services*, 1(1):1–116. DOI: 10.2200/S00176ED1V01Y200903ICR004. 11

Toutanova, K., Klein, D., Manning, C. D., and Singer, Y. (2003). Feature-rich part-of-speech tagging with a cyclic dependency network. In *HLT-NAACL*. DOI: 10.3115/1073445.1073478. 75, 83

van den Bosch, A., Busser, B., Canisius, S., and Daelemans, W. (2007). An efficient memory-based morphosyntactic tagger and parser for Dutch. In Dirix, P., Schuurman, I., Vandeghinste, V., and Van Eynde, F., editors, *Selected Papers of the 17th Computational Linguistics in the Netherlands Meeting (Leuven, Belgium)*, pages 99–114, Utrecht. LOT. 69, 83

van Gompel, M., van der Sloot, K., and van den Bosch, A. (2012). Ucto: Unicode tokeniser. Version 0.5.3. reference guide. ILK Technical Report ILK 12-05, Induction of Linguistic Knowledge Research Group, Tilburg Centre for Cognition and Communication, Tilburg University, Tilburg. 67, 84

Versley, Y. and Panchenko, Y. (2012). Not just bigger: Towards better-quality web corpora. In Kilgarriff, A. and Sharoff, S., editors, *Proceedings of the seventh Web as Corpus Workshop*, pages 44–52. 105

Voutilainen, A. (2003). Part-of-speech tagging. In Mitkov [2003], chapter 11, pages 219–232. 68

Wong, W., Liu, W., and Bennamoun, M. (2007). Enhanced integrated scoring for cleaning dirty texts. In *IJCAI Workshop on Analytics for Noisy Unstructured Text Data (AND)*;, Hyderabad, India. 81

Wu, Z. and Tseng, G. (1993). Chinese text segmentation for text retrieval: Achievements and problems. *Journal of the American Society for Information Science*, 44(9):532–542. DOI: 10.1002/(SICI)1097-4571(199310)44:9%3C532::AID-ASI3%3E3.0.CO;2-M. 66

128 BIBLIOGRAPHY

Xue, N. (2003). Chinese word segmentation as character tagging. *Computational Linguistics and Chinese Language Processing*, 8(1):29–48. 66

Yule, G. (1944). *The statistical study of literary vocabulary.* Cambridge University Press, Cambridge. 99

Yuret, D. and Türe, F. (2006). Learning morphological disambiguation rules for Turkish. In *Proceedings of the Human Language Technology Conference of the NAACL, Main Conference*, pages 328–334. Association for Computational Linguistics. DOI: 10.3115/1220835.1220877. 69

Zamorano, J. P., del Rosal García, E., and Lara, I. A. (2011). Design and development of Iberia: a corpus of scientific Spanish. *Corpora*, 6:145–158. DOI: 10.3366/cor.2011.0010. 45

Authors' Biographies

ROLAND SCHÄFER

Roland Schäfer studied Theoretical and Indo-European Linguistics as well as Japanese Linguistics at Marburg and Bochum Universities. He completed his doctorate *Arguments and Adjuncts at the Syntax-Semantics Interface* in 2008 at Göttingen University, supervised by Gert Webelhuth and Regine Eckardt. Since then, he has been working as a research assistant at Freie Universität Berlin, mainly doing corpus-based research on semantic and morpho-syntactic phenomena. In 2011, he started working on the COW ("Corpora from the Web") project with Felix Bildhauer. His teaching experience covers a wide range of topics including Theoretical and Corpus Linguistics, English and German Linguistics, as well as Computational Linguistics.

FELIX BILDHAUER

Felix Bildhauer studied Romance Linguistics at the Universities of Göttingen and Barcelona. He received his doctorate from the University of Bremen in 2008 with a dissertation on representing information structure in a Head-Driven Phrase Structure Grammar of Spanish. Since 2007, he has been working as a research assistant at Freie Universität Berlin, focusing on corpus-based approaches to information structure in German and various Romance languages. With Roland Schäfer, he started compiling corpora from the Web to overcome the lack of large, available corpora in some of the languages they are working on. He has taught courses on a variety of subjects, including syntax, phonology, semantics, Corpus Linguistics, and Computational Linguistics.

Printed in the United States
by Baker & Taylor Publisher Services